ONCE A CITY SAID

A LOUISVILLE POETS ANTHOLOGY
EDITED BY JOY PRIEST

ONCE A CITY SAID

SARABANDE BOOKS | LOUISVILLE, KY

Publisher's Cataloging-in-Publication Data
(Provided by Cassidy Cataloguing Services, Inc.).

Names: Priest, Joy, editor.
Title: Once a city said : a Louisville poets anthology / edited by Joy Priest.
Description: Louisville, KY : Sarabande Books, [2023]
Identifiers: ISBN: 978-1-956046-08-3 (paperback) | 978-1-956046-09-0 (ebook)
Subjects: LCSH: Louisville (Ky.)--History--Poetry. | Louisville (Ky.)--Social conditions--
Poetry. | Louisville (Ky.)--Economic conditions--Poetry. | Segregation--Kentucky--
Louisville--Poetry. | Tourism--Kentucky--Louisville--Poetry. | LCGFT: Poetry.
Classification: LCC: PS595.C54 O56 2023 | DDC: 811/.6--dc23

Cover and interior design by Danika Isdahl.
Printed in USA.
This book is printed on acid-free paper.
Sarabande Books is a nonprofit literary organization.

Sarabande Books is supported by the Kentucky Arts Council, the state arts agency, with
state tax dollars and federal funding from the National Endowment for the Arts.

This publication is supported by individual donors who gave to the 2021 Fund for the
Arts ArtsMatch campaign. Matching funds were made possible by the Fund for the Arts
in partnership with the LG&E and KU Foundation.

for the people of Louisville

TABLE OF CONTENTS

PLACE & PROTEST

SPIRIT & SONG

PORTRAIT & MEMORY

ONCE A CITY SAID

IN THE SHADOW OF THE SPIRES

The poets are finally the only people who know the truth about us. Soldiers don't, statesmen don't, priests don't, union leaders don't. Only the poets. . . . Something awful is happening to a civilization when it ceases to produce poets and when it ceases to believe in the report that only poets can make.

—James Baldwin

IN JUNE 2020, AT THE peak of the pandemic, I drove four days from Cape Cod, Massachusetts, where I'd been at an artists' fellowship, to my new home in Houston, Texas. The twenty artists in residence at the fellowship, including me, had been under strict quarantine by order of the Massachusetts governor for several months, but the fellowship itself had already been a sort of socially isolating, off-grid experience—designed, as it were, so that we were at the very tip of the Cape in Provincetown during its tourist off-season, between the wintry months of October and April, surrounded by the sea. Most days it was dark by 3:30 p.m. Most days it hovered around 28 degrees. I bought a SAD lamp. I walked the cobblestoned ghost streets with my dog, Luna. Then COVID hit and a fatal rush of New Yorkers fleeing to their summer homes on the Cape bloated the tiny fishing town. The only way out was through a virus-ravaged New York, so our stay was extended to June 15. When Raul—a wood sculptor I had become close with over the course of the residency—and I pulled out of the parking lot on June 13, we drove off of the physical and existential island and into an America-on-fire.

On the way to Houston, Raul, Luna, and I made several pit stops in Southern cities, where we had friends or family, to take a break from driving. We didn't realize that it would be a tour through the country's other crisis. Our first stop was Richmond, Virginia, where Raul had finished his MFA in sculpture. When we arrived, we immediately drove down Monument Avenue—its parade of Confederate statues lining the street's median, leading up to the ultimate monument: a twenty-one-foot-tall, twelve-ton bronze statue of Robert E. Lee on a horse, which sat atop a forty-foot marble base in the middle of a roundabout. Virginians protesting the murder of George Floyd just two weeks before had already torn down the Jefferson Davis statue and, in the wake of these protests, Virginia's governor ordered the removal of the Lee statue at a later date— probably owing more to reasons of safety than political commitment. As we approached the sixty-foot leviathan on foot, I was rocked by the sight of rainbow graffiti covering it like kudzu and Black children climbing it or dancing around its base. It had been claimed and conquered. The people of Richmond had said what they needed to say.

After Richmond, we stopped for two days at my parents' home in Louisville, Kentucky, where I grew up (I'd left in 2015 to pursue my career as a writer at the age of twenty-six). I timed it perfectly so that I could vote in the primaries for Charles Booker (I was still legally a Kentucky resident, after all). I knew how important the concept behind his senate campaign was: "From the hood to the holler." It had echoes of Fred Hampton's Rainbow Coalition, which put cross-racial organizing against state power into praxis, and of which Kentucky and its working-class coal miners had once been a part. As people rushed to the fairgrounds to vote, other Louisvillians gathered in Jefferson Square Park. Every evening that summer, the streets were filled with smoke, flash-bangs, and tear gas, not just over the murder of George Floyd but also over the murder of one of our own by Louisville police: Breonna Taylor.

More Louisvillians would be shot in the aftermath of Breonna's death: seven protestors were mysteriously shot during marches on May 29; David "YaYa" McAtee was shot and killed on June 1 by the Kentucky Army National Guard in the door of his restaurant business in West Louisville, miles away from the protests; a photographer, Tyler Gerth, godson of longtime *Courier-Journal* columnist Joe Gerth, was fatally shot in Jefferson Square Park on June 27, where he had been documenting the protests; and several protest leaders were harassed and killed in the aftermath of that summer—one of whom is mentioned herein, in Alissa Vance's poem "For Hamza 'Travis' Nagdy," and was shot and killed on November 23.

In Louisville—the fourth most-segregated city in the country after Detroit, Milwaukee, and Cleveland—Taylor's murder reflected the reckless and hasty disregard for Black life by city officials, especially when those lives were connected in any way to the West End, Black Louisville. Disregard for Black life is often a socioeconomic barometer of the disregard for other marginalized populations.

Before I left Louisville on my way to Texas, I went down to Jefferson Square Park to talk to protestors and to see the graffitied King Louis statue, a photo of which had been sent to me by my friend Chad Golden a few nights before. This small, condemned statue of the historically distant French monarchy didn't feel as impactful as it had in Richmond. The source of power was more obscure, decentralized, than Confederate symbols of recent historical trauma. Kentucky was, after all, a slaveholding Union state, and Louisville was on a bondsman lease system rather than the more traditional plantation system—an even more peculiar version of "the Peculiar Institution." Who was responsible for that system? Into whose hands did its profits land? In that moment— as I stood looking up at King Louis's now-handless statue—I felt that Louisvillians still had so much more to say. But, in this city, officials were not vocally supportive of the protestors and their demands. They were responding with more murder, more power, more silence.

I left Louisville unsure of how to be useful. By the time I got settled in Houston, my phone was blowing up. Writers were calling me, sending emails and poems and the damning affidavits in the Breonna Taylor case. They were telling a story about an intentionally corrupt, unchecked police department and life in the shadow of the spires— those twin symbols of our world-famous racing track, which seemed like the only thing that mattered to our city leaders sometimes, which often seemed to be made more important than our lives.

Even though I had—for the past five years—been like a balloon floating away, I had tried to stay in touch with my city as much as possible. At the same time, I was ascending further and further in my career and my book was coming out in a couple of months—my first book, *Horsepower*, which read like an elegy for the city, and a love letter, all at once. I had a platform now. What could I do with it? How could I be useful from fourteen hours away?

That July, I taught a Sarabande-sponsored workshop for Louisville writers called "Against Silence: Writing Our Current National Moment." Out of that workshop came poems included in this anthology by Rheonna Nicole, Glenna Meeks, Mackenzie Berry, David Haydon, and Nguyễn Vũ Ngọc Uyên. Yet I knew there were still so many more poets who had something to say about what was happening in our city, about who we were, and about the history of this place. Writers who wanted an opportunity to speak about the experiences they had growing up in Louisville, in the shadow of industry and tourism, but who had never had the formal literary spaces in which to share their thoughts, their art. Writers of color and working-class writers, from underserved communities like the West End and South Louisville, who felt left out or unaware of recent calls for artists' grants or literary journal submissions just as their community entered the national consciousness as yet another epicenter of police brutality, food injustice, gentrification, and the gamut of institutional problems that usually follow.

How could I use my platform to collect those poets, which included me, and bring us out from the periphery of the city's tourism and into its center? How could we penetrate the silence and insidious gentility of our city's elite?

Back in Houston, it was 100 degrees and little lizards called *anoles* slithered across the sidewalks in masses. They were sometimes the only sign of life I saw for days in the summer of 2020. I tried not to step on them and crush them under my giant foot on my long walks with Luna. Writing had led me into a space of complete isolation even though it had begun as my attempt to connect. I looked forward to the few hours on Tuesdays and Saturdays that I would spend with the Louisville poets over Zoom, trying to put language to what was happening, trying to name the unique, insulated stasis of our city, which often felt like the Sunken Place.

"Once a city said, / *How do we operationalize compassion?* before firing 20 bullets into a couple's bed," Mackenzie Berry wrote in a poem she brought into workshop (herein titled "In Which an Entrepreneur

Is the Mayor"). In the precise language of her poem, she diagnosed a previously ineffable injustice we felt at the discrepancy between Mayor Greg Fischer's campaign rhetoric and his rhetoric around the murder of Breonna Taylor, between what was happening on the streets and what was being said in press conferences and left off of affidavits. It was irreconcilable. It made us feel insane. It drove some of us to insane acts. I realized that sharing our poetry with one another over the course of that workshop and naming these old and new injustices was an antidote to institutional gaslighting and its effects on us. I realized through poems we affirmed one another's experiences. I realized that only the poet's report could tell the truth about our city, and the poets had something to say.

Kentucky is a state steeped in literary tradition, a tradition that rivals its bourbon, its horseracing, and its basketball. A tradition that boasts Robert Penn Warren—who twice won the Pulitzer and was one of the founders of New Criticism, the school of poetics responsible for how we read and teach poems today. A tradition that boasts the late scholar bell hooks, Muhammad Ali, and Hunter S. Thompson. However, there is a writing tradition particular to Louisville that has gone unnoticed. My curation here reflects that tradition, bringing together several writing communities that I have been a part of over the years, including but not limited to West Louisville poets, Affrilachian Poets, Spalding, UofL, and literary MFA poets, and borne out of writing venues now shuttered such as Expressions and the Java House—managed by my cousins at their historic mansion in Portland from the 1980s through the '00s. It was at the Java House that I read my first poems in public as an eleven-year-old girl. It was at places like the Java House and Café Kilimanjaro that Black poets and thinkers such as Amiri Baraka, Dr. Frances Cress Welsing, and our current Kentucky Poet Laureate Crystal Wilkinson came to read poems in Louisville in the early 1990s. It is my hope that we recover those poetic histories and communities in the poems that follow on Louisville's collective traditions and icons, places and protests, spirits and songs, portraits and memories.

—Joy Priest

TRADITIONS & ICONS

*It's like cleaning fish, this city, the head & eyes & spines
stripped clean to one side, all the meat to the other*

—Mackenzie Berry

Mitchell L. H. Douglas

BOP: OHIO RIVER/RIVER CITY

At the bottom, rumor has it,
is Ali's gold medal
likely nestled
next to wayward tractors,
slave shackles, & rusted
forget-me-nots of the '37 flood.

I jumped in the river
& what did I see?
Black-eyed angels
swam w/me.

City sips a steady diet
of liquid metal, faithful
citizens lining vital organs
w/gold dust tea, flakes
of oxidized orange
coating mason jar floors
like sugar grains
in libations (too sweet).

Jumped in the river
& what did I see?
Black-eyed angels
swam w/me.

At the bottom, rumor has it:
forget-me-nots of the '37 flood.
Is Ali's gold medal
slave shackles, & rusted

likely nestled
next to wayward tractors?

Jumped
into the river
Black-eyed angels
swam w/me.

JEAN RABIN GIVES AFRICA
THE BIRD

Darwin would be amazed how in your very hands dragons dissolve
into hummingbirds, dinosaurs into starlings. you made the science

of subterfuge a primary tenet of art history, painting cardinals
and the occasional pigeon in watercolors and the whitewash

of racial vertigo. but in which sketchbook are your vultures hidden?
oh, forgive me this inquisition, the great John Audubon has every

right to give Africa *the bird*, this bantam red with peacock's plume
chest puffy behind the ruffled poet's silken shirt.

it's written that Charles Darwin never gave credence to mayhem
or mystics but surely he favored the magician's slighting hand.

dear Jean, your tale's an epitome *survival of the fittest*—1-part Harry
Houdini, 1-part Ali's Bundini Brown; you, escape artist joie de vivre

prototype for Colonel Sanders—11 herbs and 4 Michelin stars
instilled in every sketch, pigments that literally drew you away

from your origins, every thin line escaping Haiti and the money-
brokers set to deny you inheritance; a favored son adopted

by Kentucky and France, you do so love being everything
but what you are: the illegitimate love child of a chambermaid

and her plantation-owning pirate—not that i'm judging! who
would choose sugarcane over Eiffel Towers? you're not the first

nor the last to sugarcoat a nativity scene. but still you do love
New Orleans, claiming the Queen's City as your place of birth,

the only place on God's Green Earth where you found (under the
auspices of debauchery) revelry for your darker strokes. but Bacchus

was never a patron saint of Haiti. Baron Samedi is your crown.
Brother Eshu Elegbara guards your gates and escape routes.

maybe there's more Dahomey owning you than you'd ever admit
to knowing as sankofa too is a bird—you could be the Bennu

of the Bluegrass! in Africa concentric circles also have their own
secret societies; you, Mr. Frontier-Ornithologist, would fit right in

as there's a role for scarecrows in all the various artforms of
Santeria. you see you've misconstrued the venerable beliefs

of your father's favorite lover to be the vulgarities of your father's
wife—again, not a judgment—but Darwin also believed in dodos

and if not in the phoenix then most certainly in its metaphor: in
the egg of your soul, John, Jeanne Rabin too takes flight; *draw that.*

Erin Keane

DIRECTIONS TO COLONEL SANDERS' GRAVE

Cave Hill Cemetery

Tell the tourists they will recognize it
by its crown: a marble bucket that spins, slowly,
to the tune of "My Old Kentucky Home,"
the world's greasiest jewel box ballerina,
flanked by sparklers crackling like manic
cake candles. Form your mouths into gentle
Os, recite the eleven herbs and spices
as we know them by heart: dried river clay,
crushed pills, pollen, coal ash, shredded
reports blackened in redaction,
rosin, jug yeast, chalk dust, pepper
balls, pole staples, errant sequins off a raggy-
hemmed gown. We will kneel and present
a coupon for a free ten-piece, it is
our custom, and receive the blessings
as they follow. By now, the tourists will have
questions. *There is no twirling bucket,*
their eyes accuse, *no dark whimsy wrought
from the dead.* True, we conjured this
tinkling fancy. There is no such thing
as a free, spinning lunch. Pay no attention
to the Confederate portraitist. Petit Trianon
vibes are all in your head. A flower for
the Greatest, a flower for the Union,
a flower for "Happy Birthday," the billing
cycle has paused. A peacock screams, a slasher
film ingénue in a brilliant, torn dress.

Join him: open the rooftops of your mouths,
dear ones, let your *yum*-s ring out like *om*.
Welcome, welcome. The swans are restless.
Please do not picnic on top of our dead.

GHOST SIGNS, FLEA MARKET

At the end of the world, the urban tortoise
knows where he wants to be: craning ancient

neck up Market Street bricks, open to catching
up with time. Hurry up & wait, he understands,

carrying the weight of home on his back
as we all do, no matter how far afield we creep.

A city can't run from itself, he knows—try it & see
how far you get. It's all a shell game—that hole

you've worn in the pocket of these jeans will never
take what you actually want to lose. He hauls

envelopes marked Return to Sender, accents,
streetcars, strains of bean we didn't even know

to miss. The silken violence of slow erosion.
We browse the booths for creased maps:

trash into treasure, so we've been told, but who
will challenge the sorting? Every day the world ends

& begins. Late or early? The wrong question.
See his shadow elongate to meet yours. Run

a fingertip across the leather of his head.

CEREMONIAL FOR THE WORLD DAINTY CHAMPIONSHIP

We honor our Schnitzelburg elders
while sleeveless men whack

played no further than this block

In the game of memory

None of us old enough to play

the stick in question a thin rod
spoil the _____ / as in
will double in price come morning

The white lines of last year's
outside Hauck's Handy Store
a slate never quite wiped clean

That neon arrow beckoning
drinks / O blessed Choco Tacos
of shotgun porches

buy your sandwich / bologna
sacrament / pickle back &

like those waxy milk cartons

For the meatless among us
blankness to contain the salt ·

from the bottoms of beer cans
a stick for sport / a world
    championship

distance is everything—

The dainty a six-inch peg
as in spare the _____ / as in
the ruin we have welcomed

game ghost away gradually
re-touched for the next chapter

buy your pull-tabs / your energy
devoured in the shadows

on white / a fifth-grade lunchbox
a bag of chips, fists of Old
    Milwaukee dripping
bought with a brass ashtray's
    scrounged change

who nevertheless need absolute
fauxlogna from the organic
    grocery

artisanal bread & Vegenaise / the shame / tell no one what
                                          you're eating

O forgive us, champions   of the ages, Little Sisters of the
                                          Poor

our fake meats & our spotless   sneakers not thrown over
                                          telephone wires

but marked up as vintage   / this hank of whatever / this
                                          analog

how it sticks in our teeth   / lingers there like pure story
tastes almost like that   which we never can miss
until we come finally home

Mackenzie Berry

MY CITY SAW THE FIRST BLACK ATHLETE MILLIONAIRE, JOCKEY ISAAC MURPHY, AND AFTERWARD THE WINNING JOCKEYS WERE WHITE

title after Frank X Walker

Off Bayly, the train tracks split
the neighborhood like a highway,
steel & rust & picks in its teeth.
On one side, the bookstore, the library,
the breakfast spot with cinnamon rolls,
housemade. The other, Lee's Chicken, the diner,
the storefront that is always changing its name.
Portland, when it was its own town, was wealthy
before the wealthy left with the river traffic & now
the shotgun houses home huddled families,
the kids stashing syrup sandwiches for school,
hauling a backpack through a screen door past
a mother's reminder of shoes on the front porch.
The smoke shops send men
with Swisher Sweets behind their ears,
past monkey bars & red slides & a swing set
on the corner & the Seafood Lady,
food-truck-turned-staple, Kool-Aid in jugs
& shrimp mac & cheese. Off 9th Street,
the highway split the city like *Maniac Magee*,
Black Wall Street turned skyscraper & hotel.
The ripping is so ripe you can taste it.
The bricks, Sheppard Square & Cotter Homes

& Beecher, Indi's & Kings with plexiglass
over the counter, faces obscured like a windshield.
Churches with lines around the block, drawn-faced men
& women shifting their weight from waiting.
Off 15th, the roads are one-way only, the buildings
closed up & shy, murals of faces & slant names
on the sides & parking lots made blacktops.
Garden beds raised on the in-betweens,
the Dirt Bowl Tournament, neighborhood squads
picking the rocks from their shoes & licking their hands,
the step teams & grill masters trading technique.
Way east, Indian Hills & Springhurst & Prospect,
where the buses don't go, lakes & streams & fountains,
picnic tables & willow trees & tee ball games.
It's like cleaning fish, this city, the head & eyes & spines
stripped clean to one side, all the meat to the other,
the hands doing the stripping swift & skilled & made to.

LOUISVILLE IS ALSO THE #1 PRODUCER OF DISCO BALLS IN THE WORLD (HOME TO THE LAST DISCO BALL MAKER)

It is debatable, so they say, whether or not the cheeseburger was, in fact, invented by Kaelin's Restaurant in Louisville, Kentucky, where it is said to have appeared on menus in 1934. It is also said that while Louisville, Kentucky, was the first restaurant to *name* the term cheeseburger, in practice the cheeseburger was experimentally created in Pasadena, California, in 1926. In Denver, so they say, the name *cheeseburger* was trademarked in 1935. Of course, while I would like to say that Louisville, Kentucky, invented the cheeseburger, it is likely that, in all likelihood, it was invented years and years before in some small kitchen with one cast iron skillet and a gas stove and some woman who wanted more, a table full of children who knew her best. While I cannot truthfully make this more than it is, I would like to say that while Louisville has never been known for poems, poetry is the act of naming, and naming is a call to act and an act in itself, and an act constitutes a thing, and therefore, Louisville invented the cheeseburger and everything before this was solely a hamburger with cheese.

Rheonna Nicole

HOT BROWN

My city has a ferocious appetite for hot browns and brown liquor.
It sits high and mighty on its brown Derby horse, gets full from its
      winnings,
brownnoses to fickle tourists but forgets about the black and brown
bodies waiting for a seat at the table.

Even now, my city still enjoys the tedious taste of Kentucky Fried
segregation, but expects everyone else to find nutrients in regurgitated
integration and opportunities from its empty Bluegrass palate.

There never seems to be enough rations
to go around but the same people are getting fed
over and over again.

I pretend like I ain't hungry though.

Eat off the hearty pieces of my pride throughout the day.
I sit impatiently waiting for more diversity-inclusive crumbs
to fall from the greedy mouth of some white man
who don't know nothin' 'bout the seasoning

in my poems. This chophouse of a town knows how to hide
the plates so well. I guess in hopes that we don't try to bite

the hand that barely feeds us. We should have just pulled
ourselves up by our bootstrap napkins and made reservations
to get some scraps from somewhere, anywhere,
just not downtown, right?

At least I can always go back to my fast-food desert.
Not a lot of substance but we make it stretch.

You know they handin' out free produce to us brown folk now.
I suppose an apple a day keeps the protests away
or the poverty away
or the police away—however that saying goes—
but I prefer a fresh batch of greens and hot sauce with my pity.

I wonder how many people I have to serve before I get a decent meal.

Nevermind, no time to be selfish
'cuz in my city we gettin' ready for Derby.
We're always getting ready for Derby.

DERBY

First Saturday in May,

> my mother wrestles my hair
> into two ponytails. The only day of the year
> she bothers.
> > The upsweep of skin
> > pulls my face into a grin.

Special occasion barrettes molded
into the white, plastic body of a horse
gallop behind me at the tip of my braids

> as I race the stretch
> of our narrow alley street,
> shouting into the mirrored windows
> > through cartoon-sized teeth:

> > *PARK HERE!   TEN DOLLARS!*

◎

Eight years old and I am a professional.

Up early to greet the regulars:
> Mr. Whitlock, Black Lincoln Town Car.
> Mr. Crouch, Red Topless Corvette.

I usher the expensive machines
into the VIP spaces of our carport,

pander through the heavy hands
dropped on my freshly parted scalp. All day long,
up and down Cliff Ave.,

I am my mother's gimmick,

reeling in the big bettors, picking the sure horse,
giving directions to the entrance
in my tiny voice, selling plots of our yard and lemonade

to orange-tinted men
sweating through linen,
their nameless women
under gaudy hats . . .

We memorize their faces
from scratchy lawn chairs,
beneath a mellow blimp
humming through the sky.

Then the streets empty.

The announcer's voice echoes,
blankets our roofs. A distant Oz.

Grills warming, beers hissing,
crowd buzzing like a radio
between stations. We wait

for the races to let out,
for our customers to stumble back
from that fortress
we've never been inside.

We argue
garage-to-garage,
placing the real bet:

                    which of us will be the first to go . . .

Robert L. Penick

DENNIS COOPER RACING STABLES

Bold Bravo, a big chestnut,
seven wins in ninety starts,
easy to walk twenty times
around the shedrow in 1980.
No one seemed to have allergies
back then, straw dust
hanging in the air
like fog.

Paco mucks the stall while
Bravo winds the clock,
hangover blacking blue sky,
missing family, home,
the past a severed artery
that will never close.

But on Thursday, if this horse
blows up the third race,
stumbles across first
among lowly claimers,
a handful of glitter
will fall on our shoulders,
something to shine
long after this summer.

Alex Shull

OUR DERBY

The cars came and filled the lawns.
The streets were clogged with limousines.
A procession of coolers and lawn chairs marched

into the gates. It felt like we mattered
to the world. And for some reason
I belonged. I was supposed to be there.
I was here yesterday and the day before.
They just came to touch our fame.

I knew where I was going—
I was going in circles
in the shadow of the spires—

I rode my bike up Longfield,
following the smell of the stables.
A giant cowboy stood watch
by Wagner's. How did he wander
so far from the ranch?

Those horses
way too small
to be his.

Get along now,

follow the twin arrows
pointing to the sky.

Glenna Meeks

AN ODE TO SOUTH LOUISVILLE

I was born on the backside
of a red brick, stained glass
Baptist church, a liquor store
on the front side.

A dusty dirt-filled backyard
back porch catty-cornered
from a juke joint. A duplex
with a bath and four rooms.

Below the bike club, a Molotov
cocktail anoint, thrown up,
bounced off my bed.
Family across the street

and alley, around all the corners,
Churchill Downs up the block.
My granddaddy was my daddy.
Born to a teenager out of wedlock.

My momma was my granny.
He brought home the chicken,
she fried it, crocheted, quilted,
kept house and raised

us kiddies. To whites we were poor,
but to blacks we were hot stuff.
Sharp clothes, fine furniture,
good food and liquor. We lived
a good life, smoking Camels and Kools.

G. G. Moore park summers sliding,
swinging, swimming. Afraid to look
out the back door when the dead lied
in wake. Kids riding bikes, chased

by gunpowder, fed dogs down screaming
streets. Liquor store snacks, dill pickles
and hot weenies. Hopscotch,
one-legged jumps, jumping rope

on sidewalks. Chalk-drawn four-square boxes,
Playing tonk and spades, scooping up jacks
on concrete porches, scraping knuckles.
We slipped into the racetrack

under barbed wire fence. Stealing
neighbors' fruit from backyard trees.
The first boyfriend and tongue kiss
in the front room. Opening my eyes

to my great-granny's gun barrel
spiriting away my third boyfriend.
My heart wept seeing a man's fist
hit the face of a woman. The sight

of someone shot in the street
made me freeze in peril.
Torrential rain flows through
my brain from threats of abandon

and slur. A communal swaddle
of neglected children we collectively

saved. Rescuing my stroke-ridden
grandmother to New York,

uprooting her. A matriarch before fifty,
from generations passing. I hear
their whispers above the vacancy
when I stand on my ancestral land.

Churchill Downs luxury boxes loom
over us, ostentatious guests party
on their bandstand. A one-way cash register
that blocks traffic from parking.

Voices yelling *PARK* are drowned out, bounce
off Million Dollar Row like fire thrown.
Two men own 90 percent of the land now,
and for us every day is the day after Derby,

empty of our lives and traditions.

Lance G. Newman II

WESTEND NEW YEAR

The crickets learned their chirrup
 after hearing the
  Westend's New Year.
No better metronome
 for the jungle
  where floating butterflies,
   stinging bees
    and sleeping snakes coexist.

The westend
 brings in the transition
  with bullets and prayers
that we don't stray.

God

made it windy tonight for a reason.

So the atmosphere would carry
 celebrations of heated metal
  away from black bodies,
for once.

The westend
 of louisville,
  where ammunition
   that bore the name
    of an opp all year,
has expired

33

and so is fired
    into the forgiving sky.

Your ears can pick up on the neighbor's caliber

as next door, often quiet,
 decides to
  "let that thang off a bit!"

The sleeping children and
 hood-like fireworks, rest
  above our heads
lulled to sleep by every victory

shot of joyous breath.

REPLACED

Louisville Slugger bats
  replaced by police batons

Bluegrass allergens
  replaced by tear gas

A 9th Street divide
  unified by Breonna's name

This year
  most murders in the city's history

Next year
  an absence of justice

A soft-spoken police chief
  replaced by a silent one

White flight
  replaced by white return
  replacing black bodies
      erasing black life

Kentucky Derby
  replaced by conversations on race

Mint juleps
  replaced by medical cocktails

Take a shot,
Wear a mask,

Pretend
    compassionate inaction

replaces our grief.

PLACE & PROTEST

The joke growing up—

we had breathed so much formaldehyde
the funeral home would give us a discount.

—Steve Cambron

Mackenzie Berry

IN WHICH AN ENTREPRENEUR IS THE MAYOR

Louisville, Kentucky

Once a poet looked to me and said,
I wish my mother had died, so that I would have something to write about.
and I have never been able to turn from it.

Once a city said,
>   *How do we operationalize compassion?* before firing 20 bullets into a
>   couple's bed
and never have the masses been able to turn from it.

Each day the tongue grows taller, and now it's almost reached the
        mouth's roof.
Each day the crowds gather louder, now nearly shaking the first coat of
        paint off the 2nd St. Bridge.

Some days I think about that poet's mother.
I wonder if there is a hum in the gutter that grows to a scream
each time she wishes her daughter a good night's rest.

I imagine all the business meetings scheduled to redraw the city maps,
all the suits smiling slightly as they ask each other which part to cut in two,
how they plot the scalpel mathematically and call this *renaissance.*

This is what a city means,
because the official statement reads [the city is growing more silent, safer]
when really it means [we are casting a mass grave, slowly]

just like the child poet who likely once told her mother,
[I'm no good at writing] when really she meant
[sometimes I dream of cutting your throat through].

Hannah L. Drake

WE WERE HERE

Originally commissioned by the Frazier History Museum in Louisville, Kentucky, to commemorate the 100th anniversary of the 19th Amendment and the 55th anniversary of the Voting Rights Act

I search for me among blades of bluegrass
dig for memories of me in fields of hemp
try to discover names among unmarked graves.

I drink a mixture of simple syrup, mint leaves and bourbon
poured over crushed ice, served in chilled highball glasses—
here in the home of the greatest two minutes in sports

they call them mint juleps. Perhaps this is the magical
concoction that will allow me to find home. So, I sip
unfamiliar traditions trying to adapt to a history

that is not mine. Feels like ill-fitting shoes on my feet.
With every step that I take back in history there is pain.
Where are the women that look like me?

Their memories and contributions to history hidden,
obscured, concealed, but these women
arc not figmcnts of my imagination.

There can be no full telling of women's suffrage
until we speak about the women that suffered
simply to have the same rights. 'Cause this is America:

the Land of the Free, which should include me.
'Cause ain't I a woman? Ain't we women?
We were here.

We have always stood on the front lines
and the sidelines. We have endured humiliation
and embarrassment. We have stood naked

on blocks and watched the world
pick apart our bodies and put them on display.
We were sold.

But we were here. We were shamed
for our appearance. We were subjected
to playing wet nurse to your babies

and therefore unable to take care of our own.
We were the conductor on the Underground Railroad.
We were here.

We ironed the shirts and pressed the pants, kept
a clean home and fought off the KKK. We made
the signs that provided slogans that would change

the world. We endured the teeth
of dogs, the brutal force of water hoses,
and the hits from billy clubs. We were here.

We assisted this nation in exploring the universe.
We started movements that changed
the very course of history. We stood backstage

as the world demanded that a man be center stage,
garnering all the credit for our work. We buried
our sons and our daughters too soon.

We endured medical malpractice
as the medical community used our bodies
for Frankenstein research. We became the face

of a movement fueled by our children's blood.
We were pioneers for freedom. We stood up
to the system. We organized. We prayed.

We fought.
We resisted.
We were here.

You do not get the luxury of erasing
our lives and our legacy from history.
We were here.

100 years is long enough for the story
of women's suffrage to be whitewashed.
Open your eyes to the history of women's

suffrage shown in Technicolor.
Open your ears and hear their names:
Fannie Rosalind Hicks Givens

Georgia Nugent
Alice Emma Nugent
Mollie Nugent Williams

Ida B. Nugent Payee
Mary Virginia Cook
Maria Stewart

Mary Ann Shadd Cary
Mary Church Terrell
Nannie Helen Burroughs

Sojourner Truth
Harriet Tubman
Ida B. Wells

Daisy Elizabeth Adams Lampkin
who said, "You cannot be neutral.
You must either join with us

who believe in the bright future
or be destroyed by those who would return us
to the dark past."

And when you remember
those names, remember the name of
Alberta Jones

Charleena Lyles
Tanisha Anderson
Atatiana Jefferson

Rekia Boyd
Sandra Bland
And remember the name of

Breonna Taylor

They were all Black
and they were all woman.
Our fight has always been

with two hands. You must know them,
you must see them, you must acknowledge
them. They were here.

Jeremy Michael Clark

STATE OF DENIAL

As though there were no North Star.
As though beneath the white oak one might find shade
    & not find oneself

dreaded from the branches.

In a front yard, on cinder blocks,
the scrapped hull of what'll get fixed
one day, one day . . .

as though the air won't keep its promise, won't turn steel
to flaking rust. As though light doesn't still fall
from something dead long ago.

There are some who like to think
this state was never divided,

as though here we don't have brothers
    with eyes & barrels aimed,

as though distance isn't the measure of everything
between us

              & what we can't see,

as though dread isn't what sways the trees,
as though one could turn away from that,

as though this wasn't the enslaved side of a river.

Joy Priest

DENIAL IS A CLIFF WE ARE DRIVEN OVER

I want to believe Don West
when he writes: *none of mine*

ever made their living by driving slaves.
But in my grandfather's mouth that utterance

would've taken on another meaning:
In the memory my mother shares,

he is flitting across Louisville
in his taxi, passing back and forth

like a cardinal, red-faced, proud-breasted,
delivering Black folks their dry cleaning—

had to, she tells me, as part of his route—
but once he started his second shift and turned

on the cab light, he wouldn't accept
Black fare. I recall him reciting

the early presidents'
racist pseudoscience—American

at its liver—to rationalize his hatred
of my father, his denial

of my Blackness. That denial a peril
I survived, a cliff he could have driven me over

at any moment of my childhood. Maybe,
I want to think, because they were poor men

who labored, farmed tobacco and dug for oil,
my grandfather's people resisted

slavery, felt a kinship with my father's people.
Or that because my grandfather

was one of eleven mouths to feed
on their homestead—reduced to dirt

across the Great Depression—
he had a white identity to be proud of, a legacy

that didn't join our names
in a bill of sale, but in struggle.

I search his surname and it travels
back to Germany, appears

on the deed to the house he inherited,
retired and died in, poor-white resentment

inflaming his stomach and liver.
But when I search the name I share with my father,

my only inheritance   disappears
into the 19th century, sixth generation:

my ancestor bred
to produce 248 offspring

for his owner, from whence comes
our family name. Mr. West, here

we are different. Here   is where
my grandfather found his love for me discordant

as the voice of the dead whispering
history. Here is where we are connected,

not by class, but blood and slavery.

Erin L. McCoy

WITCH-AUK & ME STOP OVER IN MY HOMETOWN

i bear witch-auk within the trench
of my coat all the route down the ohio,
come ashore on an island no one has claimed

beyond the blond wrecks of barges,
their haw-mouths & greedy smells.
mud furrows on her webbed toes,

she leans down to look, falls,
& the clouds snarl open their
filed teeth & the teeth fall.

all the city spins up, red blear
of sirens, we flee in all directions,
streetlamps squeal like hot plastic

but the teeth just bounce a little
& settle down. they are soft
& helix, they are the wounds

not the bullets, the walls
of a heart. the city, meanwhile,
fires thirty-two rounds.

in jefferson square park
tears orbit the ring of drains.
they are slow movers.

they are slow movers.
like a great navel filling up
with rain, so that the clouds forget

some days what they are doing
& stop to watch.
witch-auk, what have i done

but fill the river with canines
that mouthed how this was just a dream.
witch-auk says nothing,

squirms to stand back up.
her small wings tug
at just a little air.

it is enough to right her,
though the mud beneath her feet
slides her backwards into the ohio.

Marta Miranda-Straub

THE RECKONING

Louisville, KY

I awake with a brain chock-ful of infographics
woven by archetypal and historical metaphors

tattooed on the soil of my heart.
I challenge the existing violent paradigm

because all that I am, breathe, value and love
is or has been rejected, raped, shamed, colonized,

beaten, murdered or considered illegal.
I pound the podiums in public and weep in private.

I remind us of the deep wounds
on black and brown bodies,

the impotence of white dominance, and the bodies
hanging for hours from southern maple trees

while good white folks picnicked. The bodies
now lying on hallways and sidewalks for hours—

all warnings to not dare challenge your own holocaust
or seek your liberation without permission.

Often, I tremble with rage, call my skeletons
to attention, slip on my cloak of courage

and kicks for life, speak in tongues, handle
copperheads, savor the alchemy of humanity,

51

and feast on fire water, cigars
and conga drums. Today I weep in public for the loss

of decency, humanity and justice, and for all
that is sacred in our collective souls.

Robin Garner

COMMUNITY

Safe havens created brick by brick, children playing
unscathed by stigmas & statistics.
My mother cooking dinner in a kitchen
encased in concrete walls.
The four of us enthralled by adventures
of riding our bikes down south hill
& breaking one-dollar food stamp bills
for quarters at the corner store.

We didn't know that this was poor.

We knew the candy lady sold frozen kool-aid
inside of styrofoam cups.
We painted hopscotch in chalk on sidewalks,
learned double dutch with ropes.
We lived in building 40,
my cousin just over the field in 32
& my grandmother in 54.

Community.

This ain't a poem about crime scenes,
drug deals, crack epidemics,
eviction notices & poverty-stricken housing
where sometimes grass doesn't grow,
because at funerals, during eulogy,
you don't put emphasis on the wrongdoings
or justify a death, you give praise
to everything that made
what once was so great, in-depth.

These bricks bred doctors,
lawyers, judges, politicians, poets
& lifelong friendships.

These projects equipped their tenants
with the will to live & to be greater than
the expectations set upon us.

These bricks & the mortar
with which they were built
bore witness to first love & heartbreak,
single mothers doing whatever it takes,
husbands, wives, healthy black families
sustained, & the broken ones.

Culturally enriched people
driven by what was intended to be deprivation.
People with history much too rich
for demolition, or ninth street divides.

People that survive. Community.

David Haydon

BATTLEGROUND STATE, OR IN AN INTERVIEW WITH DAWNE GEE, MAYOR GREG FISCHER SAYS HIS HANDS ARE TIED REGARDING THE MURDER OF BREONNA TAYLOR

Your battle is with the state,   *not me.*

He says, as if he didn't just mention metropolitan Louisville,
politan as in *polis*, the Greek city state. Gesturing to white Athens, when
          really, he
is calling to white Spartans. Warmongers, warriors.
Cops in phalanx ready to tear
through protestors and homes and mourning.

He says as if the city is not
the state, not the State with
a capital *S*. State as in
State your intention or be
removed from this park at the commands of   *the mayor.*

As in state your open record request and be denied   denied
denied.
Denial, a permanent state of the State.

As if this isn't a battleground   state. Where white people, me
included, sometimes or all the times or times and times again say,
This is why you vote. As if a Black woman,
as if Breonna Taylor dying at the hands of the State incarnate is
a partisan issue.

As if the State doesn't charge protestors
with felonies to keep them from voting. Or charge
their bodies to the ground or into   an unmarked van.
Or as if out-of-state, State money doesn't
control the state of our state election.

As if the city isn't the same as the State. Police-like soldiers, soldier-like
police invade neighborhoods with gentrifying
bullets, each wrapped in a one-eighth sliver of a single
dollar bill.

As if the city-state didn't take a single dollar bill and split
      it eight ways to
destabilize a neighborhood, soak it in Black blood
and buy the corner of Elliott Avenue.

As if the city mayor didn't say *that's not gentrification, it's making*
neighborhoods nice for every   body so
people all around the city can have that.
A game of metropolitan   city-state   monopoly.

As if a community can belong to those outside it:
to me, to you, to a stranger looking through the
window peppered by police bullets.
Can own it.

As if Louisville's Black communities need this mayor
this mayor   this city   this city   or this state   this state
to define *nice*, when he, it, we can't officially
loudly condemn the state-
sanctioned murder of Breonna Taylor.

ON FINDING A CRISP APPLE IN LOUISVILLE'S WEST END

If a single grocery store serves twelve neighborhoods,
how does the city expect every person to eat?

And if that city plants more parking garages than trees,
does it expect apples to dangle from the garage rafters?

If apples, by miracle, grow from ceilings and not from sidewalk trees
or backyard orchards and are not for sale in a local market,

are people supposed to tippytoe or jump and pick them
or should they bring ladders?

If they can be picked, should Black Louisvillians march a couple
miles or more from Shawnee from Russell from Portland

with trampolines and ladders to garages on West Main
or 5th or 6th or 3rd or Arena Plaza?

If the garages aren't heavy with apples,
and if no one Black should be marching down city streets,

because white eyes are prone to see "riots," never injustice,
where can a young Black girl find a crisp apple

in Louisville's West End? If it falls from a parking garage,
and she doesn't catch it, does it burst into pulp?

If she does catch it, will it not already
be bruised or rotten, knocked around by traffic?

If she's hungry, does she scavenge for bits of crisp apple
or does she eat her fingernails for dinner instead?

If she eats her fingernails for dinner, do they crunch
like broken pavement beneath her feet? Remind her

of streets broken like promise after promise made
by white mayors and "neighbors," like me, to make Louisville better?

Promises to do more, secure food and water
and apply it as a salve to "save" them from violence created

by white desire to be surrounded by whiteness, to police Blackness. Our
      desire to be good,
so good we donate groceries instead of investing in a grocery store,

push cops instead of a school into an overpopulated district,
throw anything that way but reparations and support anything but
      liberation.

Does it hurt her to eat fingernails? Hurt to swallow? Does it remind
her that there is a city telling her to be compassionate

on an empty stomach? But, if she is compassionate enough,
can she pluck handfuls of dandelion greens with an applemush-sticky
      palm

from a sidewalk crack big enough to fall into, boil them, and eat
them for dinner? Or is she old enough to know that dandelion

greens picked from a cracked Louisville sidewalk are not good
without ham or bacon or lard or olive oil? That dandelion greens

are bitter. Period. Or does she eat them? And if she eats them
and is still hungry, still belly growling,

can she walk, is she in walking distance
to the one grocery store in Louisville's West End? In her part

of town? Can she find a sidewalk safe
enough to carry her to a grocery store?

Or could she even devise a maze
of sidewalks to carry her to the market?

If she makes it alive, if a car doesn't smash her like an apple
falling from the rafter of a parking garage, if she is not

a suspicion to white eyes, can she amble down aisles of apples red
as smiling lips or green as grass or golden delicious as a wrapped

chocolate coin at Christmas or pink as lips? If she plucks one
and the pyramid of apples cascades, tumbling all at once

softly and hardly and quietly and loudly
down on her, will a produce stocker pick them up,

pick her up, tell her softly that *it is okay, the apples
are okay, you are okay? They are only bruised.*

Will they tell her she is only bruised. Will she pick up a crisp, shiny
apple and take a bite as she walks safely back home?

Mitchell L. H. Douglas

AL GREEN WAS A PREACHER

before he was a pastor—
let me explain. If you can't find
a sermon in "Love & Happiness,"
something's wrong. He slides
from one strange world to the next
like Uncle Jimmy navigating his sky blue Cougar
down West Market. Al testifies
& we glide, past the Coffee Cup,
where we ate greasy burgers
in white paper, the ring & sugar
of onions steamed inside. Past
Jay's, where Momma bought my black
Chuck Taylors for first grade. Past
the Cavalier Inn, a bar
only a biker could love, peeling paint
& look-away faces. Past the Laundromat
where Daddy George washed our clothes
in big chrome troughs that ate our change,
bleached our robes.

       Al would know this world, would sing
of the corners' jut to meet you,
the pain of the angle, how one street
runs right into the next, no one
raising eyebrows. We ride deeper west, rising
out of our seats & settling back to the cushions
w/each pock in the road. Past St. Columba
where I bloodied Jay's nose in the lunch line.
Best friend, how many times
can I say sorry? Past Shawnee

where Momma, Aunt Sissy, & Uncle Jimmy
said high school is not enough. Past
empty Nehi bottles, bodies
of cigarettes bent in gutters:
what smoldered in the grip
of unknown lips, discarded
for other pleasures.

       Many a lesson waits
on these streets, like how to catch
lightning bugs in mayonnaise jars,
how to poke holes in lids
to let trophies breathe. How
to balance your weight
on two bicycle wheels,
never fall, ride
like the unfettered skip
of your heart.

Steve Cambron

RUBBERTOWN

*Rubbertown is a neighborhood in Louisville that houses a lot of
heavy industrial and chemical plants that produce acrylic plastics,
formaldehyde, Freon, and various types of synthetic rubber. These
facilities are adjacent to residential homes.*

*Aug 25, 1965: Louisville, Ky. (UPI) – Dozens of violent explosions ripped through
a Du Pont Chemical Corp. plant five miles from downtown Louisville today. The
explosions sent towering mushroom clouds of black smoke into the air, shattering
dozens of windows in buildings, and could be heard 10 miles away. Residents were
advised to immediately seek shelter indoors and to close all windows and doors in order
to block out all outside air. Residents were also instructed to turn off air conditioners
and to bring pets indoors.*

1.
       Summers smelled like cellophane melting on hot light bulbs.
We slept in sun-dried sheets, flecked with factory fallout.
Nothing in the arsenal of those cheery black-and-white laundry
       commercials'
lemon fresh, extra strength, oceans and oceans of dancing bubbles
could ever get them the kind of white they were on TV.

The joke growing up—
              if Dorothy were from here instead of Kansas,
the song would have been "Somewhere Over the *Dirty* Rainbow,"
Emerald City a sprawling skyline of crowded smokestacks.

Old Man Mcpherson, three doors down, rheumy-eyed,
undershirt watermarked with yellow sweat stains,
listening to Reds games through a pocket transistor
in a lawn chair on his porch, the gurgling

liquid cough when he laughed
a souvenir from Rubbertown, he said.

Industrial facilities and other sources can emit air pollutants from fugitive leaks,
process malfunctions and area sources that can be difficult to understand and to
manage. Next generation emissions measurement (NGEM) approaches executed near
facilities are enabling new ways to assess these sources and their impacts to nearby
populations.

("Rubbertown Next Generation Emissions Measurement
Demonstration Project," 2019)

They called us the *chemical corridor,*
they called us *cancer alley,*

Louisville's toxic armpit.

The joke growing up—
we had breathed so much formaldehyde
the funeral home would give us a discount.

Three years before Dustin Hoffman got the tip about plastics
in the graduation party aside, my neighbor, Mr. Daniels
who worked maintenance at American Synthetic,
took a brick-sized chunk of something that looked like dirty cheese
from the work bench in his garage
and placed it in my hand, announcing proudly
Boy, you're holding a piece of the future.
Synthetic rubber. No more trees. Who the hell needs Asia?

2.

On the playground at school, blacktop shiny
with afternoon sun-shower, tightrope-walking the speed bumps,
color falling through the cloud hole,
seeing, for the first time the arc entire,

red,
    yellow,
        green,
            electric beams   unblemished
                                          by smokestack haze,
a bright bridge of light curving beyond Dixie Highway,
beyond the boundaries of everything I knew—
            the rainbow Dorothy saw,
                        the kind that makes you want to sing.

3.

        Lake Dreamland, scum pond, the dream long juiced out
a waterlogged couch, half-sunken tires at lake's edge,
the rumored dumping ground for pit bulls that lost the fight,
fast-food bags, paper cups crumpled on the ground,
a NO LITTERING sign, brailled by a shotgun blast.

The joke growing up—
            if you could drink a glass of Lake Dreamland and survive
you were too damn ornery for cancer.

Heavy petting on the picnic table after dark,
kissing under constellations of factory lights,
a milky glow along the Ohio brighter than the stars,
gas flares like giant torches, angry flames
flapping in the night, a city within a city haloed
in its own hemisphere of light,
the warning signal from the smokestacks
blinking a red heartbeat in the sky.
                   My tongue
searching for the spot where hers hid,
finding only long strands of hair
snagged in braces.

Top 40 wafting from a car radio
I wish they all could be California,
I wish they all could be California,
I wish they all could be California girls.

*When I was eleven we moved to Lake Dreamland which was close to the chemical
plants and their dumps. We were evacuated on more than one occasion for chemical
leaks at DuPont. Most of the time it was from ammonia. Men would come to the
door in the middle of the night, with gas masks on, and tell us we would have to
leave. There would be a haze about a foot above the ground and it would gag you
with the smell.*

(Darleen Rusnack, Rubbertown resident)

4.
Riding my bike around the dead end circle
where we played Whiffle Ball,
counting down the laps from 100,
                                        something like thunder
from beyond the railroad tracks louder than a sonic boom.
In the sound I saw an angry giant
slamming his fists inside a steel drum.
Then I felt his fists shaking inside me, the sky
an avalanche of black smoke ascending,
pylons and power lines engulfed.

*It was scary. I was trying to warn the neighbors to get in the house during the
explosion. The air smelled like a burnt roman candle. I got a headache. The taste of
sulfur in my mouth lasted for days.*

(Leslie Pennington, Rubbertown resident)

Liar Liar funeral pyre
Rubbertown's burning your daddy's on fire!
Liar Liar funeral pyre
Rubbertown's burning your daddy's on fire!

Hours later, a screaming that sounded like torture
Anna Daniels on her knees
in the front yard as her mother struggled
to lift her from the ground. "No! No! No!"
punching through the thick stillness
of the August afternoon,

                                      a denial

so insistent it must be a spell
that if shouted loud enough could surely summon the magic
to undo what had been done—
suck all the smoke and flames back down from the sky,
draw all the scattered pieces of metal
back to where they were blown from
like Christmas gift wrappings flying back on their boxes
in the Super 8 home movies we ran in reverse
to laugh at and bring her father's green Corvair
winding backwards down the street again
safely into the driveway.

This old man, he played two
he played two till Dupont blew
nick-nack, watch your back
hear the siren moan
this old man never made it home.

5.

       On the news they said, *Worst industrial accident in the city's history,*
thirty-seven injured, twelve dead—
heaps of charred steel, girders bent
like plastic straws, fire trucks, ambulances,
a parking lot with rows of stretchers.
On the news, solemn declarations from flash-strobed podiums.

On the news they said, *This can never happen again.*
On the news, a tired-eyed lady with a bad cough
said she'd love to move out
but couldn't afford anywhere else but here.
On the news I heard a neighbor say,
You get used to it. You just get used to it.

That's all I know to do.

Bernard Clay

RECYCLING NEIGHBORHOODS

"new park duvalle"
always just duvalle
since i was born
now rebranded
regentrified
a sugared outer shell
of pastel vinyl cloned homes
on postage-stamp lots
crowding and dashing into
interstate-obstructed horizons,
barred in by the shadows
of coal ash smokestacks
here backyard gardens
grow out of the rubble
of plowed-over projects

southwick and cotter homes projects
a fifty-year experiment
i grew up adjacent to
named for the white developer
who always owned this land
and the black mayor
of the town sacrificed
for this monstrosity
of terra cotta buildings
knotted up and down
the single potholed street
dead-ending
at a police station
where cops were soldiers

doing tours of duty
in *that little africa shithole*

"little africa"
sometimes called "black parklands"
other times "needmore"
forgotten hamlet of freed slaves
self-governed
self-educated
with planked streets
brown brick businesses
wooden cottages crammed
and cobbled to the river
community growing
like an orange trumpet vine
from the bogged black earth
of this once bypassed marsh

ignored avoided swamp,
nameless estuary
too many mosquitos
too much stink
to do anything here
back before emancipation
before beargrass creek
became our sewer
and it still flowed
through the middle
of what is now downtown
feeding enough fertile sediment
to build the first louisville upon
before corn island, too,
got all used up by this city

leaving only a spangle of stones
visible when the ohio river
is shrunken by drought

IROQUOIS PARK

on some fall saturdays
after hours of being trapped
in a prison of droning
designed to shame me
mom broke norms and sabbath
we'd leave the stained-glass early
invite my bff to sleep over
pick up a box of wings and wedges
from indi's, avoiding dad
for the afternoon
and heading out to that mound
south of the city

after eating, while mom lay on
the picnic table and read long
neglected *jet* magazines,
laron, vette, and i approached
that hulking hill before us
that we likened to a porcupine-
leviathan, like the one that ate jonah

and we ran full speed at it
got swallowed behind its jawless row
of tulip-poplar teeth
and let the dense honeysuckle
seize us deeper into the belly
of those woods
we kept charging through and up
to its limestone-blowhole-lookout point
to view the skewed city spiderwebbed out
to every horizon

then we'd chute all the way down
the persian rug of gold
and orange leaves on our backs
the city and everything else falling away
eventually getting down to mom
my eyes thunder stormed
my shame gone

then we'd go home
and if   sports were off
and if   daddy's teams had won
then right before snl's cold-open
he would give laron and me
the *whose-daddy-makes-*
the-best-popcorn? quiz
we'd answer *you do, of course!*
that newfangled microwave corn
of laron's suburbia
couldn't stand up
to daddy's hot-out-the-pot
masterpieces
each buttered and salted
handful a crunchy blessing

Nguyễn Vũ Ngọc Uyên

MY SOUTH END

Years ago my dad promised we would buy a house
near the library, because I loved books.
My mother bought that house for us eventually in Beechmont.

Before Beechmont, my South End was Taylor Boulevard.
I watched the Derby goers parade once—rich and poor
alike strutting down the street in their hot pink, blue and lime green
suits and feathers and heels pouting against the concrete,
because rich or not, winners or not, they all are reduced
to walking on their own two feet.

Cars zoom by so fast down Taylor; they don't want to see
the man on the corner, sign saying, "Anything would help."
Bus stops housing sallow faces, paying in changes we can't afford—
rent rising, cars broken in, people dying, librarian
pleading—save the youths. Hold the guns. Even
the needle exchange van keeps moving.

Before Taylor it was Americana,
the apartment complex that housed new immigrants and refugees.
We were taught, tell the bus driver "Americana"
and he'll bring you home. Americana
is now a community center, once founded to serve the complex's
residents.
Americana Community Center took its name and moved out,
still serving immigrants and refugees.

The East Enders gush about South End's diversity in ethnicity,
but
they don't live here.

They know and love Vietnam Kitchen. But
do they know Thuy Van, A Chau, Chilakiles, La Riviera Maya and
La Guanaquita?
Diversity is more than one.

Tree-lined Southern Parkway is so green—
envy well watered with silence—muffling buses hissing by on all kinds of
streets—except the prettiest part of the boulevard, where sidewalks stretch
wider than houses just the next block over.
Only there can the aging poor and the newly welcomed afford to live.
We can all hear the 1 a.m. fireworks months after the Fourth of July.

Everyone's favorite is Iroquois Park, where Southern Parkway meets
Taylor Boulevard, where Beechmont meets Iroquois, where the
middle class meets
no one.
I wish people would love Iroquois Library
as much as Iroquois Park, where
you not only see people, but also meet people.
There, Sophie Maier, the city's first Immigrant Services Librarian,
will tell you,
"Say hi" and "Come help."

The Beechmont folks complain
on the neighborhood's Facebook group
about the area's diversity
in income and struggles,
and "the homeless,"
and strangers knocking on doors.
A stranger knocked on our door:
"Your mother's garden is beautiful."
My mother is never shy at saying hi.
Our neighbor shared his patch of garden with her.

She was the first to know his name. My mother
moved away last year. This year the patch is still
sprinkled with purple tía tô, and amaranth still
snuck in between his kale, cherry tomatoes and muskmelons.
"Someone left free aloe plants in the Woodlawn gazebo," my mother
texted.

My neighbor said, "My mother used to know everyone on this street and
all the blocks around."
I worried when he and my brother talked about shooting whoever stole
his mowing equipment. Some Beechmont folks planned Black Lives
Matter protests on Southern Parkway. Cars honked driving by our signs.
My neighbor's daughter raised her fist in solidarity. The next day, their
door window said ACAB. She loves books too.

NEIGHBORS

In the beginning,
Pat told my mother she could plant anything she wanted next to his
vegetables.
Then some of the tomatoes that lay sunning on his porch moved across
the driveway onto ours.
Zucchini, yellow squash, okra followed.
Pat can't eat it all, but he keeps growing them, she laughed.
Beans, cherry tomatoes and peppers too showed up in our kitchen.
The most prized were the orange squash flowers, in soup, with garlic,
stuffed and steamed.
Pat said I could have all the flowers I want. I gave him some stuffed flowers and he
said they were good. Here, bring Pat some of these eggrolls.
In the years that followed Pat kept growing squash, "Because your
mother likes them flowers," and the string beans she likes, and the
peppers in Pat's yard keep getting hotter because jalapenos weren't spicy
enough even though Pat's stomach can't tolerate spicy things
Because our family liked them that way.
Then we moved away and Pat's still there growing
His Beechmont garden extending into the front yard
Rows of tomatoes, cucumbers and asparagus beans behind a wall of
unapologetic sunflowers eight feet tall
Inviting visitors and Instagram likes.
There's a farmer's market on Southern Parkway, I offered.
He laughed, *I just give them away to people who walk by*
And the sunflowers. I guess the women like their flowers.
Yesterday Pat texted
Tell your mother in about three days the okra will be able to pick, maybe 7
She's missing out a lot of flowers from the pumpkins.

Lately I've been thinking a lot about food and people
And I dream that Louisville is also a garden,

Green vines generous with squash flowers eager to be plucked to fill the city's
12,000 bellies that don't get enough to eat
And the spoon doesn't ask if you're truly hungry or where are you really from.

§

Writer's Note: When my family first moved to the Americana Apartment complex, I kept having these dreams that if I could just cross the invisible fence between our apartment buildings, I'd be right back in Viet Nam. In the past quarter century, the American dream has been pushing those homecoming dreams further away. And now I'm stranded in a land beyond my mother tongue, my tongue slightly thickened with a Southern accent that only people outside of Kentucky hear. *Hiraeth* is a word more familiar than I realized.

Ken Walker

AS PRESTON STREET MOVES SOUTH TO HIGHWAY

Turn right off Hoertz
Almost immediately cut off Number 43

Next—left on Shelby past Dairy Del—big
Pepsi logo faded to a rose-indigo plastic matte

Shelby ends its one-way posturing
Here Preston flows automatic

A specific type of 90 in this kind of July—
Moisture tends to be magnetic—allows
no escape—the apex of the southeast

Must be much worse somewhere
like Georgia or Tennessee—how
count your blessing implies a stacking
of gratitude you can withdraw from some
inevitable someday when it may be worse
but that will never come to be sweetheart

Pass three cemeteries in Audubon
before the cemetery where my grandfather
and uncle are buried—next to Male Traditional

Stop—park—say hello to the packed rock
Donnie was a drinker but a very loving father

Once said   *If I did not have Danielle*
it'd've been a lot sooner

Fondest take on Jack—seeing him
cannonball into a pool at 61

Same day he tried grilled fresh squash for the first time
That was the day before he died

Graffiti on the marble block glass window
of the carpet store nearby reads   *Zaybo rubs*

Every fast-food restaurant
you could imagine
sometimes even repeats itself
along this stretch—white folks complain
that Latinx folks have taken over

But in all honesty this
is the least boring and tastiest
the Central to South End has ever been

Mostly flat save for a few little knobs

Farther from the river but you can still feel its breath

Closed and boarded up Shell station near the Outer Loop
Seems to symbolize parts of the world ended years ago

White bubble graffiti on the side
of the building reads   *I'd rather not*

Nothing at all natural about these 10 or 15 miles
Not many places you would want nor could linger

In the nineties it was cruising
Daytons—Lacs—tints—Mister Gatti's
I remember Mia X
From the windows of a navy Buick
Leave a bout it scarf on your face

Way down now—make a left on Mud Lane
Another left on Brooklynn Lane—ironic now since I spent
a third of my life bouncing from Fort Greene to Park Slope
to Bushwick to Flatbush to Prospect Heights—now right
on Arroyo Trail where my grandparents lived—shoddy
post-midcentury neighborhood
slacked in split-level homes—elms and chestnuts
seem to have grown taller—Baptist church sign reads

Separate but never far away

Distance propagates out here near the county line—once went
for an off-road race in a car my parents lent me—
tire marks all through the farm of an unknown neighbor—destroyed
the drive train so much that the steering wheel
had to be turned 180 degrees in order
for the car to go straight—transmission stopped working
altogether immediately—if I think *we* in this sense I think
Bergson's notion of open totality as in opposition to herd

Learned that night that we not only forgive whiteness
the easiest but white children the most—

Baseball fields and park on the right reads   *Optimist*

Remember the red jersey and white pants—cleats
and high socks—can feel that fifteen-year-old
giving up on sports competition—caring more about being loved—
acceptance from whoever would give it—

Did not really know
how yet to give it to myself—now
man sitting alone in a parking lot
in front of the short cinderblock
Tractor Supply building
behind a table next to a large cooler—

Sign says   *T-Bones and ribeyes*
                             EBT accepted
                             Best meat south
                             of the south end

I drive up
Buy a few ribeyes and thank him
for being here—he says   *I'm the only black man*
                             you'll see for miles that way
                             and points toward Shepherdsville

I laugh with him and thank him again
The numbers have not changed
for Okolona or Hillview—almost feels
like a collective secret how diverse
it actually is—even though it all flows
from The West in this town—cars
and road expansion gave whites our wings
and those kind of white wings
are the one-sided kind—where wings
and recessions prove the visibility
of abandonment

Ananya Roy essay in passenger seat reads

                             Setting everyone apart
                             while bringing them together
                             like a magnet in a slow fire

                             Slumdog cities make microfinance
                             an inherently racist act

So many signs stripped of their lettering—plywood exposed

More liquor stores than libraries

Not quite enough medical centers

Gathering places are the small cobbled together
houses—apartments—under the overpasses

Buses hardly arrive

Sandwiched between used dealerships—mechanic shops—
tire shops—gas stations—check cashing outlets—every once
in a while a pop-up college—coin dreams—

Mimicking vast mountains
out toward Tioga—Jefferson Memorial
let the imagination roll through its own negative space

When Thomas Bullitt presented himself to the Tsalaguwetiyi
he said he was there as a friend and a neighbor

When Frederick Law Olmsted heard
in the past that slaves were made to swim across
the Ohio—to see who had the best endurance—
he supposedly vomited on the banks of the river

A letter Olmsted wrote to the great-great-granddaughter
of Thomas Bullitt reads

*Honesty   means looking further
into everything without cause and without cessation*

Straight back up through the light at Eastern Parkway
passing White Castle and the post office

On the radio is an ad for the reopening
of the Muhammad Ali Center

Right on Forrest
Left on Texas

Park car—walk into cool air

makalani bandele

EAST BROADWAY, OR ON CATCHING TARC (TRANSIT AUTHORITY OF RIVER CITY) UPTOWN

one way to talk about mass transit is in verse. but then the heart must be
traveled and inconspicuous enough to take, at any one time, one of over
seventy circuitous routes with all their stops and turns. there is a center
in a city, a locus from which

all the buses begin their runs, poetic lines, to
push exigencies point to point—to another denied territory further west
than the average commuter is comfortable.

the simple wish simply to go forth in words. and it is not that simple
where most of the buildings have black eyes and broken teeth. where
folk walking the streets are little tax dollars so small as to be invisible as
the moon during the day. they have no business in any part of the city,
and whichever way the city goes, they get run over and drug behind it.
it's hard enough to get words to visit, nevertheless stay here. the center
cannot hold. such hardship so concentrated and so continuous, terrifies

the majority onto the expressway
that is a belt around the city. panic takes them to the clunk of the inner
and thud of the outer rings of the suburbs, the sidewalks don't cut a
path, the streets are cliché, and all the chemlawn has killed the cicadas.

but board an eastbound twenty-three at any sheltered stop below ninth
street, and a vibe will feel you for a ride through down-
town. a girl from guadalajara moves over so you can sit next to her.
across the aisle, a man and his daughter giggle about the skittles they're
eating. behind you, the stench of stale, cherry-sweetened cavendish, as
dude guts a black & mild. an old woman with a grocery cart and an
old man, who has a trash bag half full of something in one hand and

an enormous dictionary in the other, get on. they are differential orbs
among all the frowns. in the many faces, you can see we are still fighting
the civil war. the center cannot. the bus swings wide. it's crazy how these
big buses can make such sharp turns. you keep pulling the yellow cord,
to everyone's exasperation, in hopes that people will get off, and new
people will get on. this is probably as close as you'll ever get to effecting

any kind of change in people.
if nothing else you love the anaphora until you reach your stop.

disembarking onto the empty street corner, it's cold. you make a pair
of scissors with your fingers and mash the spaces between each digit to
tighten your gloves. heading south, only the police and landlords know
where smoketown ends and germantown begins.

SPIRIT & SONG

I love nothing
more than the damp field behind my teeth, where a stable-
boy turns loose the wild horse none could break.

—Jeremy Michael Clark

makalani bandele

FLEUR-DE-LIS

sidney bechet bought an old, beat-up soprano saxophone, when it is
difficult enough to play one that's in tune. he was gallant like that; when
he was so inclined, he planted petite fleur in quiet imaginations. similar
to the way he might enter a blossom, wrap himself in the bouquet, buzz
his malediction, and retreat to paris, a pilgrim sets out on a journey to
find her holy place, an ice cube wanders discursively along an aqueous
path till it has fully realized new liquid form; this i am sure of, if only
because i am myself a b7 minor, sanctum, and slowly melting. what line
is not after another? what note either in a lucent solo? railroad tracks
run from east coast to west coast and back, the train takes the tramp
wherever she wants to go. at some point she will find herself along the
banks of the ohio in a river city looking for lost treasure—a gold medal
tossed into a great waterway by an ex-patriot. the lilies in this city have
no sweet odor for they are made iron, and rust with time. the meter also
changes—it is in the variation of timing and stress that a feel is created
that gets the whole storyville jumping. and while the cathouse wholly
throbs with vice, poets make the polite music of the middle class. you
can make poetry whorish, but you can't make it unpopular. a breeze
stumbles in on this gruesome scene and pets the wilting yellow iris in
a vase. she is a flower of basin street, her occupation is to be known,
and known often well. why do we try so hard to be beautiful, when we
already are? he was rough, and before she knew it was all over, her little
flower was gone.

Anna Leigh Knowles

AFTER EVERYONE IS GONE

Behind Wagner's white barn and Wayside Park
    freight cars brake the lidded silence of sleep.
        Against the tracks, a chain-link wraps to the side
            of our duplex. Fragments of plastic bags trill

behind the concrete bench swirled in gray rose
    where scattered gravel grips the grass path toward
        the house as the birdbath and sundial slant
            in dead nettle. Lilacs warm with noon,

and in the backyard, a charred hole drops
    into some dark, opened oval where the fire bin
        burned through spring. Everything Bud and Laverne
            saved was set to flame over the hole after they died—

ticket stubs, calendars, bus tickets. They saved ledgers
    from past decades, thimbles from countries visited
        by train, stained coasters from Louisville to New Orleans.
            A tax business moved in last November,

and when there's nowhere left to go, I drive by
    and cut the engine—let the air aim my thoughts
        over all the years I'll live. I feel like saying, *Dead,*
            what do you want from me? It comes out

wrong. Along the tracks, I watch as bands of crepe
    myrtles hold nothing but black wasps bounding
        in sweeps like buttons dropping from large coats
            and behind that, saucers of diesel blow from semis

downshifting past Kroger. I hope to be cut loose too, if only
    for a while, the way erosion has blurred the flatland
        clay of the riverbank miles out. There's more
            to knowing myself than haunting the backyard

as though it were a tomb. There has to be trust in an origin
    story. When I tell this one, I need to mention the sickness
        binding me to this place by blood. I know the reason—
            I'm starting to consider how when the wind

moves, all human truths outlast their own decorations.
    Even as the chimes toss, even as they heave,
        the screen door becomes an ache in the hinge
            of the jaw, silhouettes flit one place or another.

THE PAST DOESN'T BURST INTO SONG
LIKE IT USED TO

Too much anymore to write
into rooms that were never mine.
The afternoon assembles below
the power lines where the Pepsi billboard,
upright and alight in its giant aluminum
can, wavers above the highway.
All there is, ever was: shadows
of branches in a windowpane
thrown across the floor, its one
watery eye. This bouquet of half-
finished history recedes, expands,
like riverbeds. Whir of beaters
downstairs before anyone opens
the door to let the trains in.

Ryan Ridge

DRUNK AND LONGING IN LOUISVILLE

I parked cars for a living as my life stalled out and worried way too much about Y2K. I partied like it was 1999 until 2002. I couldn't start a sentence without talking about myself: I. By then, most of my friends had either married or moved to Portland, Oregon. This was before Portland morphed into a television show. Me? I stayed true to 502, hanging around my hometown, and hitting every other bar on Bardstown Road every other night. Germantown, too. Most days, I slept past noon and when I rose it was like a bottle rocket as my afternoons exploded into nothing. I played chess against the computer a lot and lost. It was an anti-education, even though I learned to work the crossword puzzle in pen while unemployed. These were the war years: Bush the Younger and his heavy friends. God had split town for another it seemed. We braced for the worst and expected worse. I didn't know what to do so I stayed half-drunk and oblivious, kept a loose tongue and a can of mace. Back then, you could still make mistakes. Still, I knew I needed something long-term: a plan, a partner, the possibility of a pension, a pet, a change of scenery, and fast. I thought a lot about Portland or Austin or Brooklyn, but never did it. Instead, I sat at my crooked kitchen table in the Highlands and smoked sixty thousand cigarettes while listening to Will Oldham, Silver Jews, and Slint. Eventually I landed in Los Angeles, which didn't amount to shit. Now I live in the mountains and try not to look out ahead.

Jessica Farquhar

NEW MOON TO-DO LIST, OR, I LEFT MY BEST SEASON IN LOUISVILLE

That crying, it is just middle-of-the-night crying.
In the hierarchy

of complaints, it is the one you can ignore.
I cannot ignore

Will Oldham. I have a weak spot for anyone
who plays

Cupid. I have a weak spot for Will Oldham, but not
a soft spot.

The new moon means you have nothing,
not even starting

from scratch because from scratch implies
ingredients.

It is frustrating having nothing, and it might make you cry.
Just be careful.

What you wish for might explode as stars sometimes do.
And if Will Oldham

would just pull an arrow out of that quiver
in his voice

I just might fall in love again with something. I just
might find something.

Today all I find is nothing, but there is a river
I can float down

to another town, and Will Oldham is there.

STEAD

Your trucker hat, your no hair under there;
will our marriage be

a merger or I am acquired. All the houses
have painted themselves

manicured what's outside, and I thank them
for the little

gradients in color and scape
the movement

in hue from blue to white
and back.

As the moto-passenger I am all trust
& daydream

while I steady the bike singing your songs
inside my helmet.

I think you will you will be me someday
when I become you.

Aileen Tierney

FEBRUARY 15TH

Tomorrow, I will walk myself
over the sidewalks with little penguin-steps
past the branches fossilized with ice,
and buy the most expensive
luxurious box of chocolates in the sales aisle
and heap half-priced hydrangeas
already dying in my arms,
the florist giving me that pity-smile,
telling me to be safe out there.
But tonight, I'll finish this bottle of beer
so I can break it over my head,
then call my dad.

David Higdon

CERAMIC JESUS

The day Dad reclaimed his faith he brought
home a ceramic cross to hang on the wall,

two-dollar sticker stuck on its base
and crude initials scrawled in the back.

The wood was painted a patchy acrylic,
a brown too dark for the wood of a cross,

maybe a railroad tie or a jungle vine,
but not the wood cut by a Cross Maker.

My father watched men beat each other
on TV in our dim-lit living room.

Under that cross, I'd watch the boxers
lock up, wrap long arms over shoulders,

slick with sweat, a cut over a swelled eye,
the bell signals the end of a round, retreat

to corners, sucking the air, spitting teeth
into a metal bucket. The ring girl would circle,

a bold number held high. Eyes and howls
from the smoky dark. Bloodstains
and dirt, and Jesus staring down.

Joy Priest

WINNING COLORS, 1988

I am born in the season of color-blocking & crack,
in the dawn of the Reagan era. The light & dark
shades of *School Daze* dance across movie screens.
A girl-horse wins the garland of roses.

554 blooms sprout red around her roan neck—shock
of black mane, haze of white down her nose.
Before her only two fillies clutch
the purse: Regret, 1915; Genuine Risk, 1980—

our names for girls.   When my birth horse
sets off out of the gate, a man & woman are working
their eleventh hour, twirling around the country club,
in the graceful choreography of weathered

servers. The woman, just 12 weeks pregnant,
not yet swollen with her dark choice. The man
taking bets & slurs alike out of the mouths
of the club's members—rich & red-faced from

mint julips. When the woman hands off dirty glassware
to the man, father of her child, she giggles, smacks
him on his great black ass. When the girl comes down
the last stretch, she's been out in front the whole race,

foal of Caro, violencing the dirt.
Expectations stamped into bets, at one point
her odds: 100-1. When her neck clears the wire
into the known world, the dark trumpet sounds.

Robert L. Penick

MIDNIGHT AT THE QUARTERPOLE BAR AND LOUNGE

Drunk, stumbling, I walked down to be with the other humans. I treasure solitude but, on this particular night, darkness gnawed at me like cancer. Halfway there, an older Hispanic man rolled up on his bicycle. Asked where the nearest tavern might be. He rode ahead and I met him at the Quarterpole. We watched the people dancing, laughing, coughing, swearing, drinking, carrying on with a manic desperation.

They were racetrack workers: grooms, exercise riders, hot walkers. All of us poor. Owners and trainers must drink across town, I told my friend. His name was Gregorio. Said his boss couldn't win a race if he saddled Secretariat. Just before last call, he leaned into me and whispered, "Everyone here is missing a piece of something. The sad ones laugh too much, unhappy lovers cling like skin to bone. The poorest players buy the most rounds. Everyone hides a secret. What is yours, my friend?"

Jeremy Michael Clark

ONE YEAR SOBER

Can't say I miss that

          beach where on every walk I burned

                   my feet

that time the swarm

            of wasps took over

     the church

Each day was once

       a bitterness I couldn't bear

              without a drink

was once a glass

door smudged by everyone

who ever left

I was a plastic cup

rattled & filling with whatever

others could spare

The future just a model

home I couldn't imagine

calling my own

If a cluttered desk

emptied by a sweeping hand

can be considered cleaned

I suppose it was

sometimes peaceful

                                    how a drink could clear my mind

Now at night I count

            the planes above & trace

                                    the path that brought me

    here

            to this house

                                    where restless in the dark

    I stare at that familiar spot

            on the wall: those newly laid bricks

                                    in the shape of a door

SOUTHERN DRAWL

Here is where the bloodhounds tried to dig up
what's rested in the dirt. Before dawn, I searched
for what haunts me & found I'm a man after my own
shadow. Who could stand to hear a tongue forged
into shape? Someone says *mastery*

                                    & I hear *misery*.
Cracked lips, I wish you a wetting. I love nothing
more than the damp field behind my teeth, where a stable-
boy turns loose the wild horse none could break.

Isiah Fish

I WILL TELL YOU WHAT JOY IS

At the barbecue,
Jordan, who once
said he wouldn't
ever have gay friends,
compliments the canary-
bright manicure on Slim,
who's clad in feathered shoulder pads
like a red-winged blackbird
switching downwind,
& Jordan says, *I see you shinin' boy*,
& the birdsong chaperones
the deejay into dusk
as sunlight blushes across
the cranesbill-bloomed field
& the nest of niggas chop it up
like old-time love-battered chums
beneath the pavilion
where the wild swift moon
& Slim's Tommy Girl perfume
hypes the whole crew
when they glide in the pulse
of Electric Slide like one band
of brothers achatter
in the absence of sirens.

Alissa Vance

FOR HAMZA "TRAVIS" NAGDY

There is no air in this room
Technically, maybe, there is
But it doesn't belong in my lungs
There's something off about this oxygen
I don't think it was always like this

The sun rises differently too
It doesn't soar anymore
It just listlessly defies gravity
Slowly and steadily climbing in its arc
Across the sky

Hamza, my lion
It is you I follow across the sky
You weren't a shooting star
I saw the Milky Way in you
A whole bright night infinity
I tell myself that we didn't lose you
When you were set free
You are not gone

Just back floating among the stars
I still see you
We still hold your memory here
Folded like hands in prayer
When I blink, all the water falls out of the air
And I am submerged in this river of grief
Again,
I can't go on

No, the wise mind says to my child mind
Do not turn around
You are not going that way
There is a way forward and we will find it
My chin trembles but I keep it up
I can't go on, I'll go on

Hamza,
I find you in the North Star
I hear your chant in the beat of my heart
Keep going
There's a vision that can't be
Unless we are here to realize it
Keep going
For you, Hamza
With our prayerful hands, we will build it
We just have to
Keep going

This air still doesn't taste right
But I'll keep breathing

And the sun may rise differently now
But if it can rise still
Then I can too
Then you can too
And we can find the way forward together

V. Joshua Adams

THE WAY OUT IS THE WAY THROUGH

It's dawning now, in the green afternoon light,
you've been mistaken for someone else.
Look around: the street is empty and silent,
houses in their motley of potted flowers and hanging ferns
salute each other like old veterans.
A lizard scrambles the tile of a Juliet balcony
under trompe l'oeil blue. Nobody's fooled.
There's no confetti, no photo op, no book signing.
There will be no calls to the radio shows,
no disarming the hosts with unpretentious banter.
Obviously schools, street signs, and plaques
are out of the question, since there will be no scandal
followed by a sufficiently contrite interview
with a tough but tender anchorwoman,
the one who wrote the book about being raised by nuns.
Hardest to accept will be the lack of encomia
delivered grudgingly by rivals
to their biographers long after your death.
Most days you just ask unanswerable questions
to audiences too streetwise to believe
there are no answers. And when you are not doing this,
you are peeling ginger or dusting the bookshelves,
or washing the household underwear.
Or taking mountains of boggy cardboard
out to the sticky bins. There, on the ground, you find
the wonderfully spherical nest, with one small, sandy egg
still inside. How long can it last—no, it's already gone.
Nothing of yours remains either, unless
someone catches here something of themselves,
and, before moving on and forgetting it for good,
thinks it's better this way, to be no one worth knowing.

Kristi Maxwell

FROM "STROLL"

a pedestrian sonnet

*

How a cut makes it seem blood's so anxious to get out.

Reading the word "curiously" at the moment "curing" pops up occurs?— in a reminder (Check curing garlic—may need another week).

To have reservations—but where or about what/whom?

The fountain with its slim fingers of water that make it look like it's scratching the sky with its obvious welts.

A tree with sudsy clusters gathered on the glassy skin of its leaves.

A few houses side by side with stones arranged like turkeys or someone holding and fanning out terrific or terrible swords of light.

Where the painted crayon looks like a condiment bottle more so than a crayon, "We build our kids for the future" rather than a future for "our kids."

He knows the yucca, I know the poppy.

Dairy Del, it turns out, short for Dairy Delicious—we walk through the drive-thru when the walk-up window is closed.

Duct tape encircling the bicep of the tree one learns is a gypsy moth caterpillar barrier, an insect a misguided artist made into a pest.

Eight rolled rugs set out for junk day, pattern-in, but we don't stop, so we don't see the patterns.

A house the color blue water never is, a flower the color of a house.

To call the new cardinal a "little dude" doesn't seem fitting, but neither does your hand as a provisional nest, so you just go with it.

Here, the porch stairs are designed to be welcoming, widening toward the road, giving the impression of opened arms.

FROM "STROLL"

a pedestrian sonnet

*

The thing that had changed was your decisions.

Paramour or paronomasia?—that both speak to a doubling, to a disruption of an illusion of containment, i.e., the pun is a punk, inherently, in its rejection of stability, in its brazen infidelity, a marveling in displacement—and the human aspires.

An account of psychic geographies.

Eyes best described as "bulbous" or as blood blisters.

The ubiquity of a rice grain, that it can operate as a unit of measurement: "Ideally, the hairs will be the length of . . ." in order for the wax to attach.

Pumping stations at Reservoir Park don't help with dismantling the Earth Mother metaphor.

That's a long green, unlike a long face—an efficient car stops & starts & startles.

An eventless countdown.

Toothy shadows, biting at an abstraction in the concrete.

A reminder that cities become rather than are.

What is the tensest tense?

You compromise on a mile, and he speaks the last quarter in German you forget, again, he knows.

It would've been alright to live, he says, before trailing off—a cicada shell he lobbed still clinging to your dress.

O dark brooch.

PORTRAIT & MEMORY

Someone lit a cigarette,
it is 1970 again.

—Ellen Birkett Morris

Sunshine Meyers

FRAIL

A cigarette left unattended
still burns.
Its white ashes hold
their shape as long
as they can and
I think I have been
that cigarette before.

Ellen Birkett Morris

WHERE THERE IS SMOKE

Someone lit a cigarette,
it is 1970 again.
I'm home, an apartment
with overflowing ashtrays,
too few bedrooms
for my sisters and me.
My mother drinks coffee
all day. My father, cola.
Blue smoke wafts toward the ceiling.
There is silence or shouting.
When we move, after the divorce,
pictures come down to reveal
white rectangles on yellow walls.
The slow staining of years. How easy
it was to become accustomed to misery.

ODE TO KENTUCKY

after Kevin Young

I want to be drenched in flour,
11 herbs and spices,
and deep fried.

I want to wander through
the deep green hills
listening for God's voice

to tell me when to shoot
the deer, and go home to
watch enough basketball

that I forget all the players
on my team are white boys
in their own special fraternity.

I want to take my OP 30
in peace, smoke my cigarettes
anywhere I want, wander unmasked,

watch the ponies run, and when
they stumble go back to the bar
for a beer and a bullet.

I want my wife to look
like a beauty queen, while
I stare at the girl at Dairy Queen.

I want everything
to stay the same
forever.

SPORT OF KINGS

My father's ashes are in a black box on the mantel in my living room. The exterior so like the dark leather jacket he wore on the streets of Detroit as a teenager. The box, though heavy, hardly seems big enough to contain him, his boundless anger, unquenchable desire, all of those big dreams. His brothers took handfuls of ashes to sprinkle on racecourses around the world. To be trod on by thoroughbreds. The sport of kings, the poor man's hobby. Part of him ferried in the groove of a hoof over the finish line, at last a winner. Part of him here, tethered to the family he didn't know how to love, who love him still. Love him enough to make space on the mantel, touch the box as I pass, remember the muchness of him, the bigness, his power ground to dust fine enough to blow away in a stray wind.

Steve Cambron

WHEN THE WIND CAME

*September 14, 2008: Remnants of Hurricane Ike moved across
the Ohio Valley. For two hours wind gusts of 60–80 mph were
common across the Louisville area. Over 400,000 homes in
Louisville lost power. It was Louisville's worst power outage ever.*

The storm swelled like my father's anger,
slow to rise.

Grocery bags fat with air
rose and sank over rooftops.

Orange recycling bins skated
down empty suburban streets.

Kids playing on the sidewalk
spread their arms, leaned into the wind

and instead of falling,
remained locked in place, as if gravity

had gone to sleep and forgotten them,
or, turning around, felt the bluster

at their backs bully them forward.
Trees bowed to buried roots

as if to touch the place they came from.
Neighbors stood on their porches

hands to heads like visors,
staring at the sky for signs.

No green-gray anvil clouds,
no siren's fanfare ever came.

The trees offered their small branches first
as if to appease the storm,

then big limbs took the power lines down.
The weatherman's vectors and arrows

could not predict the exact crack and fall—
which houses would be guillotined by the violence

of broken oaks. We huddled
in our basement while the world outside our walls

shuddered and groaned. In the morning
chainsaws whined through the city

the sky purged to perfect postcard blue.
Our roof had made it through.

But something inside felt different,
as if the foundation had cracked

and shifted overnight leaving us to wonder,
in that eggshell hush of aftermath,

just how long our home would hold.

Joy Priest

ABECEDARIAN FOR ALZHEIMER'S

Angel was my pappaw's girlfriend when he died.
Back there, in my memory, I hear my mother fussing about
condoms & *AIDS!* she is saying, *the girl is 25 . . . & Black!* My
daddy, amused at the irony of racism, whispering to me: *He's at his
end anyway.* Angel was stripping at Déjà Vu when he moved her into the
front bedroom & this is where I began to realize what, precisely, was
going on: he couldn't remember me, but by then he was forgetting who
he was too. Outside the club, next to our world-famous horseracing track, the
infamous sign read: *Win-Place-Show Bar | 99 Pretty Girls & 1 Ugly One!* A
jab at Angel—their only dark-skinned dancer. She mystified them with her
kaleidoscope of color contacts & quick weaves. They loved her *equine* legs. I
loved her for telling my secret loud, for making a messy joke of him & my
mother the way I felt they had made a mess of me. After Angel moved in, I
never saw him again. My mother avoided his street. She could not get
over the hypocrisy: How he'd disowned her when I was born, then made her
promise not to speak of my Blackness, my father, to me. Buried hole of
quiet lies they dug for years before it opened beneath the two of us &
ruined everything. Maybe my mother envied Angel because she
saw the truth of him out & when he began forgetting
to hate us, to put his white hood on every day, Angel
used him the proper way. I like to think of her as
Veritas, the goddess of truth at the bottom of that empty
well, naked & holding a hand mirror. Or maybe it was me, a
xeric unblooming thing down there beneath them. I had, for
years, been taught to live that way: Black, unassuming,
zipped up in history—a disease not even progress can cure.

Lance G. Newman II

HERITAGE

My heritage was lost
        in a Texas textbook.
I'm not sure
        which tribe these
    features came from.

"Almuma Molo,"
I don't know my people.

Tooklo, Dewe, Lago, Jola,
Solahola, Mandeg, Soza,
Kordobolo and Olof.

Family trees cut down by
 colonial deforestation.
   Forced immigration.
    Ethnic amalgamation.
       Cross continent pollination.

What strain did my seed come from?

Am I the strange fruit
 unaware of where
  it was pulled?

Grew ripe
        with a tongue
    that never fit my mouth.

"Xaamalekul Molo,"
I recognize my people.

Tooklo, Dewe, Lago, Jola,
Solahola, Mandeg, Soza,
Kordobolo and Olof.

I tried to find heritage
  at a retail store.

Learned being black
  is expensive.
    Shown being African
      was poverty-stricken.

Then I understood:
  the poor look rich
    to keep from looking
African.

My heritage was tailored.

Seams
  torn apart at Gorée.
Fabrics and prints
  that looked like
        passports.

Identifying my heritage

Has been hard in these
        rags.

"Tobaba gore rafet na,"
    You look good
in white man's clothes,

in white man's politics,
in a white man's uniform,

My heritage was erased
           torn
ripped   fragmented
           broken   hidden
L
        O
                 S
                          T

And now I seek to create
my own.

"Dama wara delu ker ga leegi"

Aileen Tierney

OLD LOUISVILLE

Puffy dogwood boughs
wag blooms on pavement, like fists
of coarse wedding rice

Jasmine Wigginton

GROWING HANDS

After my paternal grandfather left the segregated army of western
      Europe he came back to Kentucky
using his GI bill to learn farming methods for working fields that did not
      belong to him.

He was a sharecropper, using his hands and skills to tend to broad green
      leaves of tobacco.

Their roots sucking nutrients out of the dirt and leaving cracks in his hands.

Sometimes leaving the countryside, he would go to Louisville to work in
      segregated tobacco factories.

*in the corner of my apartment, a peace lily wilting its leaves yellowing, the stalks bending
to gravity, and my ignorance of their care.
my cat nibbles at its fraying ends.*

Eventually, he settled in Louisville, in Alpha Gardens, a small subdivision
      built
by a black man for black families, streets away from the shacks that once
      sat in Little Africa.

In his backyard, on his land, he made his Eden.

On his land, his hands picked plump tomatoes and snapped green beans,
      grew beets bright purple
pickling them in mason jars. Eventually, their crisp ridges sliced through.
      Their juices
colored the tan kitchen counter.

He now owned his relationship to the land.

i trim the dying leaves, move the plant around the living room to different forms of
        light, and try to water
at the plant's discretion.
we do not speak the same language.
working the root is my lineage—birthright.
but i am disconnected.
maybe my hands are choosing to forget. wanting to unlearn what was forced onto us
        after we crossed over.
so, they are killing this plant.

In his backyard, he would take me out in the hot summer months. I
        would work alongside him
in his garden with complaints foaming from my mouth.

Even though my words did not show it, I was happy to spend time with
        the person that made me feel safe.

While I walked alongside him, complaining about the heat, he arched
        his back, suspenders sliding down, and perspiration coating his lips.

My grandmother placed her laundry on the line outside to dry in the
        summer breeze.

He arched.

I complained.

The clothes blew in the wind.

plants are sentient beings they feel pain and respond to their surroundings in ways
humans think
we understand. the vibrations of soundwaves stimulate their transfer of nutrients
causing them
to harmonize their natural rhythm with the sounds we have created.
they listen to us.
i play my peace lily "strange fruit." maybe then it will understand my relationship to
things that grow.

Now, the rows of black dirt, formerly manicured, are covered with grass.

Unattended and forgotten.

John James

KENTUCKY, SEPTEMBER

My grandfather stood outside smoking,
watching the migrant workers
bend over the bare furrow.
I was in the cross-barn stripping leaves
from green stalks, knowing God was cruel,
that he must be. Even on a map
South America looks like a sick heart.
I hung the leaves from tiered poles
and let them dry in the heat.

Once we found a she-goat dead,
her belly split, and blood trailing over
an arched rock. Something about
her innards spread across the ground
made me think of nakedness.
My grandfather took the carcass
in his arms and carried it to the driveway
where I said a short prayer.

Stripping finished for the night,
I sat next to my grandfather
on a wooden bench behind the barn,
hands beneath my legs, our backs
cocked against a bale of hay.
Bats erupted from the silo like buckshot.
Then I realized this wasn't my grandfather,
and these weren't my hands.
All of this was a pasture resembling heaven.
Heaven was a meadow in time.
The moon rose over the empty fields
wedging shadows together in the dirt.

YEARS I'VE SLEPT RIGHT THROUGH

The field is steeped with the violence of horses.
Night descends blue hills
and I attempt to weigh distance,
as a calf tests its footing to the water hole.
On the front porch, my cat devours a hummingbird.
He beats the brilliant body with his tufted paws.
He breaks its wings,
swallows whole the intricate bone-house.

Inside, the pilot light is burning.
My sister's friend with the coal-eyes is over.
Gradually, I crawl into bed, aching for more light.
In the dooryard
a young boy stoops to pluck
feather from feather until his hands are sore.
So prone to sadness, this thief—
I take my glasses off and lay them on the table.
The shadow of a tree rests inside my palm.

This spring I commemorate my father's death
by tacking deer-horns above the door.
My hammer-strokes disperse
an assembly of hens,
waiting around for me to scatter their seed.

A mile away the river is abundant.
It breaks its sudden excess
on a limestone bridge.
A big-axled wagon tips into the water,
where white mud washes the coachman clean.

This is a custom he repeats every year,
coming and going until his wheels give out,
coming to wet his tongue.

Dawn chalks over the horizon
rendering the sky a storm-blotched red.
The outline of a cow appears on the hill
and then dissolves into the fog.
I follow her path with my ear,
listening as a bell sounds out the trail—
It is mine, this world
of bread and skin and stone.
Lay me in the field with all the fallen horses.

THE MILK HOURS

for J. E. J., 1962–1993
and C. S. M. J., 2013–

We lived overlooking the walls overlooking the cemetery.
The cemetery is where my father remains. We walked
in the garden for what seemed like an hour but in reality must
have been days. *Cattail, heartseed*—these words mean nothing to me.
The room opens up into white and more white, sun outside
between steeples. I remember, now, the milk hours, leaning
over my daughter's crib, dropping her ten, twelve pounds
into the limp arms of her mother. The suckling sound as I crashed
into sleep. My daughter, my father—*his son*. The wet grass
dew-speckled above him. His face grows vague and then vaguer.
From our porch I watch snow fall on bare firs. Why does it
matter now—what gun, what type. Bluesmoke rises. The chopped
copses glisten. Snowmelt smoothes the stone cuts of his name.

Martha Greenwald

OFF DWIGHT ROAD

One deer, jew-eyed, old, stares from a neighbor's yard,
chewing lawn. All day he's stood to monitor our work

until the minivans, stuffed, extruding mold, crouch
in the driveway, lowriders bound for a nightmare rally—

Skip the tricked-out rides—we've packed a half century
of saxophones, Lionels, madras ties. Find the '39

World's Fair ring, greened souvenir to turn my thumb
gangrenous. 1,000 feet away, the Parkway thrums, frantic

with holiday traffic. So much like my father, long-faced,
anxious, the deer worries that his cronies, bored back

at Exit 114, will get brazen, dart into an express lane,
enthralled by chrome ignited in November dusk.

Who stole father's sense of irony—the Hungarian
who watched him catapult across the hood, lodge

in the windshield, then fall, smashed on macadam?
Does the deer look to me because he's my father?

Identity literal; don't dare question this appearance.
Envy the doe, who rises from these woods on lovely

dancer's legs. Together they chaw acid yellow leaves,
joke a bit. In the middle of New Jersey, the hunters

& predators have gone, so herds seek clearings,
fields, thickets to rest in, to rest upon. The deer claims

   minor trees behind foreclosed cul-de-sac chateaus.
We watch him limp & scuffle toward the curb.

   "Listen," he says, "my four legs are killing me;
Jews were not meant to walk on cloven hooves."

DOUBLE AORTIC ARCH

For Lucy

Yes, the kid who mocked her was a jackass,
   slumped in the back of AP Psych, pecking

at his cell like a scab; yet when he heard
   my daughter's mucosal hack, then broadcast

to the classroom, *y'all belong in a home for dying*
   coal miners, somehow he'd sensed her dolorous

cough (its weird, dark timbre) portended
   backstory—not the Paleozoic echoes

of his papaw's blackened lungs, but historied
   nonetheless, boggish & primordial.

She was just 6 weeks old when surgeons repaired
   her vestigial vascular ring—& the 9-month

clamp round her trachea left artifact—a secret
   comma of cartilage that entraps secretions—

sounds to make strangers scatter & trigger fright.
   Although each doctor predicted full recovery,

Poseidon, our cardiology intern from Athens,
   offered prognoses I treasured most. His rounds ran

dawn to dusk. He entered & left our ICU room sunlit.
   Such a name—embroidered in teal on his lab coat,

no trident, just a stethoscope clacking as he bent
　　to listen. Who could doubt him? Despite her raw

scalp IVs & pale-pink chyle snaking along tubes,
　　he'd proclaim she was *strong kid, strong kid,*

then I'd cross to the windows & stare down an alley
　　where a '37 Louisville flood high-water plaque marked

the block. I swear I saw cast-iron buildings immersed
　　to their filigreed parapets, a dull sun attempting

but unable to set beyond the bloated Ohio, brackish
　　silt so full of 50-million-year longing for mornings

when leaden seas were all the sky could recall.
　　Behind me—lopsided gurgles of phlegm, ancient

waters drained from cisterns—my daughter,
　　coughing as she slept, supine in a tilted glass crib.

Sarah McCartt-Jackson

AUTOBIOGRAPHY

I was raised

by a wolf
to make hay
from the dead
up from the bluegrass

alone with a ghost who lived
inside my stuffed dog's eye

with a rod, with a shadow, on top of a streambed
over a pall, with a slice of quartz stuck
in a seam.

—

It is the age of:

pipe-ash holes in his sweater, the sigh
of a timbered hill, its slag-heavy charcoal breath
almost like a campfire, but with a belly full of wet rot

an iris bulb, wilded by departure.

—

My birthplace

is a clutch of crabapple
is a clutch of crocuses, tiny bulbs like fish eyes

the inside of a half-rotted limb they call a widowmaker
and inside that limb's papered nest.

—

We are called

spoonwood, kingcatchers, blade of anonymous grass
hickory nut, poplar, Allegheny serviceberry
sandstone, quartzstone, granite, marble, slate
a stone without a name.

—

After sunrise
turn the thing over in your hand
read its crease, its unbreakable line.

What would you do with a block of salt
made from the former life of a woman
who couldn't stop herself from looking back?

—

The new moon

keeps its face like the underside of a tails-up penny in a parking lot

keeps its face like the dark inside of a fist

keeps its face like a lighthouse, always looking away
toward another shore that it will never get to.

—

The year is

a corpse's hair that keeps growing in the coffin:
a myth, a lie, though what kind of lie would that be?

It's the wreath made of a daughter's hair, hung on the wall when she
      left.

The look of a daughter's face as she's leaving
her eyes turned back when you call her name.

This year is the door latch clicked into its plate.

Anna Leigh Knowles

WHEN MY SISTER TOLD ME TO LET HER ALONE

There was a gun—the dumb luck he kept tucked in a drawer
      without a key, covered with cross-stitching of cartoon birds,
          baby feet, tiny periwinkle x's sprouting into little girls

whispering into cupped hands. All I heard on the phone
      that summer was my sister slurring in the kitchen
          while cabinets slammed shut like trunks.

Whispers so her boyfriend wouldn't hear.
      As if I couldn't recognize it, the ugly in his talk,
          as if a scream wasn't buried in me somewhere, waiting

to stumble from my mouth. Even if she'd vanish
      for a second behind the clothesline into ablutions
          of yellow light, he followed like a tin can trail scraping
          his frown

up and down their dirt yard yelling her name. The river was full.
August and too much rain greened the windows of my sister's car

overgrown in weedy bluestem for over a year. It broke down.
Brakes thin, steering shot. Wheel stuck in a singular stiff turn.

There was no money to fix the battery.
Tents pitched in yards. Porches gaped wide,

mattresses leaned against walls like entrepreneurs
while Louisville became the ransomed sore in her throat,

a sweltering mirage between the blur of bridges.
Barges wore down to an oily film stretching along I-65

like dirty fingerbones under whose steel
spins of timber lurched and turned.

Her boyfriend was jealous and I was afraid.
A few days in a row I waited on the end of the line

whispering, *Walk toward the river, come on, walk,*
but that afternoon I stood in a room three hundred miles away

in my sister's hand-me-downs,
so sure I could be useful. I wanted to save her

but that would be unhealthy. Too many times I believed
        the gun in her mouth. I could see it, opening
            her mouth wider, wider still. Her eyes

skimming the ceiling, looking for the feet of angels.
She loved him. Night after night I saw her die—

smelled the orange shag swathed
        with the scent of heady plums. Heard the piano
           he bought for her 28th birthday, shut up

in the back room she played nights with no one home
        singing some motherless, nerve-split tune.
           A house of prayer, the heart-engraved face of Christ

withered to the walls. There was nothing I could do.
        Goddamnit they were alone
           with each other and the dark day shafted

slow sun through the iron porch swing
        like arrests of dank air, fanning out
                like money in a bankrupt home.

Seed-heavy jays shook power lines.
Neighborhood dogs prowled the fences and groaned in blight.

In the evening, her man called from her phone
and I was so happy, I thought my sister escaped

to the safe side of the river alone, standing tall in the sun
with her dark hair streaked to her cheeks with good news

of escape. *Stupid-yapping-bitch* was all he said.
But I always knew her voice was somewhere

behind his chained throat, back with the tomatoes
she tended like children lost in the vines where her heart

beat slow. She loved it there. Watched over the plants.
Stepped on the stingers of dead bees. This was new,

my sister turning her back to me. She was in love.
My hands have never been more useless—I hated him, I hated him

for making me reshape her body in all the costumes of air.
Water roped swollen vines, sludge thick.

The river hurled slick slabs, dragged what didn't want to be dragged.

ROSES IN THE EYES, OBLIVIOUS TO THE THORNS

Here is a family lined up like a jury.
      Behind the peeling garage, red letters

scrawl over a white sash that spells
      Kentucky. Behind that sash

is my uncle, fist clutched to the band,
      smiling down as though at a baptized

baby. Another scrap of sash tails off
      as my grandmother raises the edge

enough to read *Derby*. She shakes
      it back and forth. My mother is nearby

in loose jeans, sweater ruffled as clay
      mudflats. Bangs curled inward

like a hand on a steering wheel.
      My father sits in front, the teenager

from Detroit in Louisville. Banners
      flap over his head. He is a jean scarecrow,

out of place for Kentucky spring.
      What do I do with the photo's whispering?

I've held it too much and each time,
      they all live the same hundred lives.

I've slept in its stasis, folded beneath
        my pillow as though it would hatch.

No one speaks, usually. Facts blur
        into fantasy. But today, they live

inside a season of wishful thinking
        stretching on and on. All they want

is to win—to jockey each eager gamble
        into one plea: *It can be.* Wagers scatter

around years swirling into focus.
        Laverne's skirt is hard to make out

in the sun cutting through the chastened
        syringa, what runs there—stitched horses

in different strides circle the hem. Me,
        not yet whole-bodied, yet to cash in

on May's plump prize. The years
        are slow to pass, heavyset. In the distant

future—the face of a girl who gawks
        at others, a gleaming shard, a self

calling across aphids. No matter the roses
        in the eyes, oblivious to the thorns.

Jessica Farquhar

BUCK-SHOT

There is a mess I have to live with,
the dross of a coalhill
someone might mistake for what I meant
to take with me.

When, at the time, there were two
of everything, what I took
was half exactly. In the shed, in the deep
freezer, we put

our heads down to see what was left.
Venison remnants
from some bucks shot. Now that's
what I've got.

It was like someone died, and it was like
I inherited. It was
like there was a flock of belongings and
I flicked it.

Darcy Cleaver

OWENSBORO, KENTUCKY, LATE LAST JUNE

The road rolls and dips along lines of beans, hills of corn,
tobacco, wheat. Beautiful, an hour ago.

Now, my bike chain's dry, cell phone dead, and I sweat
like no lady should. The water tower, my blunt compass, is long gone.

These backroads loom with frothy-mouthed dogs, chiggers, and rank
      strangers.
Shotguns pop somewhere near. I whoosh pass the rifle range sign, pocked

with bullet holes. Almost miss the fat man cleaning fish.
Y*ou're a far piece away.* He points his blade. Might as well say, *Git!*

I'm thinking of my boys when I flag down the truck,
the world they'll inherit, how I don't want them afraid.

Tires crunch on the gravel shoulder. But he's all hat. No English.
The next truck's rooster red. The driver's arms are inked and ropey.
      Dice tumble

inside my chest, luck or snake eyes. As he lifts my bike into the back bed,
the scorpion on his bicep strikes. Below the elbow, Mary's tattoo-blue
      eyes weep.

I open my own door and see them in the jump seat, two little girls,
their lips pinched and curious, just like his. *Where to, ma'am?* He straps in.

Wind, wheat, risk. Killdeer on the wing.
My water tower. It's beautiful again.

THE POETS

V. Joshua Adams is the author of the poetry collection *Past Lives* (JackLeg Press, 2024) and the chapbook *Cold Affections* (Plan B Press, 2018). Work of his has appeared or is forthcoming in *Bennington Review*, *Posit*, *Painted Bride Quarterly*, *Tupelo Quarterly*, and elsewhere. He teaches literature and writing at the University of Louisville.

makalani bandele is a member of the Affrilachian Poets. He has received fellowships from the Kentucky Arts Council, Cave Canem Foundation, Millay Arts, and Vermont Studio Center. He is the author of two collections of poetry, *hellfightin* (Willow Books, 2012) and *under the aegis of a winged mind* (Autumn House, 2020), awarded the 2019 Autumn House Press Poetry Prize.

Mackenzie Berry is the author of *Slack Tongue City* (Sundress Publications, 2022), a poetic reckoning with Louisville and the South. Her poetry has been published in *Poetry Ireland Review*, *Up the Staircase Quarterly*, and *Hobart*, among others. She received an MFA in Poetry from Cornell University, where she teaches. You can find her work at mackenzieberry.com.

Steve Cambron's poems have appeared in *Literary LEO*, *Word Hotel*, and *Heartland Review*. His poetry has been set to choreography by the Louisville Ballet and has won two Green River Writers awards. Cambron is the creator and host of Flying Out Loud.

Jeremy Michael Clark's work has appeared in *Poetry*, Academy of American Poets' *Poem-a-Day*, *West Branch*, *Southern Review*, and elsewhere. His manuscript was recently a finalist for the National Poetry Series and a semifinalist for the Cave Canem Poetry Prize. He is a therapist and lives in Brooklyn.

Bernard Clay is the author of *English Lit* (Swallow Press, 2021). He received an MFA in creative writing from the University of Kentucky Creative Writing Program, and is a member of the Affrilachian Poets collective. His work has been published in various journals and anthologies. He currently resides on a farm in eastern Kentucky with his wife, Lauren.

Darcy Cleaver is a teacher, poet, and playwright. She received an MFA in creative writing from Spalding University in 2022. Her work has been published recently in *Transom Journal* and performed at Commonwealth Theatre. She lives in Louisville with her wife.

Mitchell L. H. Douglas is the author of *dying in the scarecrow's arms* (Persea Books, 2018), *blak*\ *al-fə bet*\ (2013), winner of the Persea Books Lexi Rudnitsky Editor's Choice Award, and *Cooling Board: A Long-Playing Poem* (Red Hen Press, 2009), an NAACP Image Award and Hurston/Wright Legacy Award nominee. He is a 2021 National Endowment for the Arts Creative Writing Fellow, a cofounder of the Affrilachian Poets, and Associate Professor of English at Indiana University-Purdue University Indianapolis.

Hannah L. Drake's work has been featured online at *Cosmopolitan*, the *Bitter Southerner*, *The Lily*, *Harper's Bazaar*, and *Revolt TV*. She was named a Daughter of Greatness by the Muhammad Ali Center. Drake was honored as a Kentucky Colonel, the highest title of honor bestowed by the Kentucky governor. Her website is hannahldrake.com.

Jessica Farquhar is the author of *Dear Motorcycle Enthusiast*, a chapbook published by The Magnificent Field in 2020. She holds an MFA from Purdue University, where she was the assistant director of Creative Writing. Her work has been supported by the Kentucky Foundation for Women.

Isiah Fish is a queer poet and performer from Louisville, Kentucky. He holds an MFA from Southern Illinois University Carbondale where he worked as an editor for *Crab Orchard Review*. His work has been published in *Albion Review*, *Blood Orange Review*, *Foglifter*, and *Miracle Monocle*.

Robin Garner is an award-winning poet, spoken word artist, facilitator, creative, woman, and mother. She utilizes her passion for poetry and spoken word to uplift, encourage, and ignite her audience.

Martha Greenwald is the founding director/curator of The WhoWeLost Project, and the editor of *Who We Lost: A Portable COVID Memorial* (Belt Publishing, 2023). Her first collection of poetry, *Other Prohibited Items* (Mississippi Review Press, 2010), was the winner of the Mississippi Review Poetry Series. She is the winner of the 2020 Yeats Prize for Poetry. Her work has appeared in *Slate*, *Poetry*, the *Sewanee Review*, the *Threepenny Review*, and *Best New Poets*. She has held a Wallace Stegner Fellowship and been awarded fellowships by both the Kentucky and North Carolina Arts Councils.

David Haydon is a essayist and poet from Kentucky. David is currently a doctoral student in the Creative Writing and Literature at the University of Southern California. His work explores Southern queerness, maternity, and significations of the body.

David Higdon's writing has been published in *Appalachian Review*, *Still: The Journal*, *Exposition Review*, *Rust + Moth*, *Wild Roof Journal*, *Black Moon Magazine*, and others. He is the 2021 winner of the Kentucky State Poetry Society's Grand Prix Prize. He lives with his wife, daughter, and son in Louisville, Kentucky.

John James is the author of *The Milk Hours* (Milkweed Editions, 2019), selected by Henri Cole for the Max Ritvo Poetry Prize. His poems appear in *Boston Review*, *Kenyon Review*, *Gulf Coast*, *PEN Poetry Series*, *Best American Poetry*, and elsewhere. Raised in Louisville, he is pursuing a PhD in English at the University of California, Berkeley.

Erin Keane is author of three poetry collections as well as *Runaway: Notes on the Myths That Made Me* (2022), a memoir in essays, and editor of *The Louisville Anthology* (2020), both from Belt Publishing. She is editor in chief at *Salon* and teaches in Spalding University's Naslund-Mann Graduate School of Writing.

Anna Leigh Knowles is the author of *Conditions of The Wounded* (Wisconsin Poetry Series, 2021). Her work appears in *Blackbird*, *Memorious*, the *Missouri Review* online, *storySouth*, *Tin House* online, and others. A recipient of an Illinois Arts Council Agency Award, she has also received honors from the Appalachian Writers' Workshop and the W. B. Yeats Society of New York.

Kristi Maxwell is the author of eight books of poems, including *Goners* (Green Linden Press, 2023), winner of the Wishing Jewel Prize; *My My* (Saturnalia Books, 2020); *Realm Sixty-four* (Ahsahta Press, 2008), editor's choice for the Sawtooth Poetry Prize and finalist for the National Poetry Series; and *Hush Sessions* (Saturnalia, 2009), editor's choice for the Saturnalia Books Poetry Prize. She's an associate professor of English at the University of Louisville.

Sarah McCartt-Jackson is the author of *Stonelight* (Airlie Press, 2018), which won the Phillip H. McMath Award, Weatherford Award in Poetry, and Airlie Prize. Her chapbooks include *Calf Canyon* (Brain Mill Press, 2018), selected for publication by Kiki Petrosino, *Vein of Stone* (Porkbelly Press, 2014), and *Children Born on the Wrong Side of the River* (Casey Shay Press, 2015). She is the recipient of an Al Smith Individual Artist Fellowship from the Kentucky Arts Council, and has served as artist-in-residence for four National Parks. She is an elementary school teacher in Jefferson County.

Erin L. McCoy has published poetry and fiction in *Narrative*, *Conjunctions*, *Pleiades*, and elsewhere. She holds an MFA in creative writing and an MA in Hispanic studies from the University of Washington. Her work has appeared in the *Best New Poets* anthology twice, selected by Natalie Diaz and Kaveh Akbar. She won second place in the 2019–2020 Rougarou Poetry Contest, judged by CAConrad, and was a finalist for the *Missouri Review*'s 2021 Miller Audio Prize. Her website is erinlmccoy.com.

Glenna Meeks is a poet and filmmaker from Louisville, Kentucky. Her poems have been published in the *London Reader* and *TAUNT*. She lives in New York City.

Sunshine Meyers is a self-professed Louisville native, speech-language pathologist, artist, and closet poet. While these titles may seem disparate, they each convey her primary passions of communication and self-expression. As a bisexual woman and survivor of long-term abuse with PTSD, Sunshine aims to use her poetry to embolden the voices of others who are all too used to living in silence.

Marta Miranda-Straub is an Afro-Caribbean queer woman and member of the Affrilachian Poets. Her bilingual memoir, *Cradled by Skeletons*, was published in 2019 by Shadelandhouse Modern Press. She has performed at multiple marches and venues including the Nuyorican Poets Cafe in New York City and the Speed Art Museum in Louisville, Kentucky.

Ellen Birkett Morris is the author of *Surrender* (Finishing Line Press, 2012) and *Abide* (Seven Kitchens Press, 2021), poetry chapbooks, and *Lost Girls* (TouchPoint Press, 2020), an award-winning short story collection. Her poetry has appeared in *The Clackamas Literary Review*, *Juked*, *Gastronomica*, and *Inscape*, among other journals. Morris was a finalist for the 2019 and 2020 Rita Dove Poetry Prize. Her poem "Abide" was featured on NPR's A Way with Words.

Lance G. Newman II is the recipient of 2022 Bill Fischer Award for Visual Arts. As a playwright, he helped create plays such as *The Smoketown Poetry Opera*, *The Westend Poetry Opera*, and *The Blood Always Returns*. Under the name SpreadLovEnterprise, he teaches his creative writing and public speaking curriculum in schools, community centers, and organizations. He co-hosts the largest and longest running poetry slam in Louisville and is the executive director of YoungPoets of Louisville.

Nguyễn Vũ Ngọc Uyên is a Vietnamese American immigrant, a social worker, and a therapist. She lives in South Louisville with her husband and their two cats and two dogs.

The poetry and prose of **Robert L. Penick** have appeared in the *Hudson Review*, *North American Review*, *Plainsongs*, and *Oxford Magazine*, among others. His forthcoming book *The Art of Mercy: New and Selected Poems* from Hohm Press, his latest chapbook is *Exit, Stage Left* from Slipstream Press (2018), and more of his work can be found at theartofmercy.net.

Ryan Ridge was born and raised in Louisville, Kentucky. He is the author of four chapbooks as well as five books, including *New Bad News* (Sarabande Books, 2020). His writing has appeared in *American Book Review*, *Denver Quarterly*, *DIAGRAM*, *Passages North*, *Post Road*, *Salt Hill*, *Santa Monica Review*, *Southwest Review*, and elsewhere. An assistant professor at Weber State University in Ogden, Utah, he codirects the Creative Writing Program.

Alex Shull is a longtime Louisvillian and lifelong poet. He is a software developer and has two children.

Rheonna Nicole is a poet, artist, spoken word competitor, and entrepreneur. Rheonna has been a featured speaker at the National Council of Negro Women's Martin Luther King Jr. brunch, Girls IdeaFest, Kentucky Women Writers Conference, and Indiana University Poetry Festival. She has been featured in *Today's Woman*, *LEO Weekly*, *Insider Louisville*, the *Courier-Journal*, and Spalding University's Art and Literary Hotel. She is founder of Lipstick Wars Poetry Slam (a partnership with ArtsReach of the Kentucky Center for the Arts).

Aileen Tierney is a native of Louisville, Kentucky. She received her BA from the University of Kentucky and is currently a doctoral student at the University of Iowa, studying contemporary literature and digital humanities.

upfromsumdirt is a poet, visual artist, and author of two full-length poetry collections, *Deifying A Total Darkness* (Harry Tankoos Books) and *To Emit Teal* (Broadstone Books), both released in 2020. He is a 2010 Kentucky Arts Council Al Smith Individual Artist Fellowship recipient.

Alissa Vance is a community activist, poet, and writer, born and raised in Louisville, Kentucky. In her daily life, Alissa fights for housing and racial equity, freedom and liberty for all people, and justice still for Travis Nagdy and Breonna Taylor.

Ken Walker is the author of *Twenty Glasses of Water* (Diez, 2014) and *Antworten* (Greying Ghost, 2017). His work can be found in *Boston Review*, *Hyperallergic*, *Poetry Project Newsletter*, *Brooklyn Rail*, *Seattle Review*, *Atlas Review*, *ANMLY*, and elsewhere.

Jasmine Wigginton is originally from Louisville, Kentucky, and currently resides, works, and is in school in Baltimore, Maryland. Her writing has been featured in *Marquee Louisville*, *TAUNT*, and *Root Work Journal*. She is currently working on a collection of writing centered around ancestry and Louisville with her uncle, poet Bernard Clay.

ACKNOWLEDGMENTS

V. Joshua Adams

"The Way Out Is the Way Through" previously published in *Ariadne Magazine*.

makalani bandele

"fleur-de-lis" previously published in the *Louisville Review*.

Mackenzie Berry

"My City Saw the First Black Athlete Millionaire, Jockey Isaac Murphy, and Afterward the Winning Jockeys Were White" first published in *Up the Staircase Quarterly*.

"In Which an Entrepreneur Is the Mayor" first published in *The Lumiere Review*.

"Louisville Is Also the #1 Producer of Disco Balls in the World (Home to the Last Disco Ball Maker)" and the two poems listed above previously published in *Slack Tongue City* (Sundress Publications, 2022).

Jeremy Michael Clark

"State of Denial" previously published in *Scalawag*.

"Southern Drawl" previously published in *Poetry Northwest*.

upfromsumdirt

"Jean Rabin Gives Africa the Bird" previously published in *Deifying A Total Darkness* by upfromsumdirt (Harry Tankoos Books, 2020).

Mitchell L. H. Douglas

"Bop: Ohio River/River City" and "Al Green Was a Preacher" previously published in */blak/ /al-fə bet/* (Persea Books, 2013).

Martha Greenwald

"Off Dwight Road" previously published in *New World Writing*.

David Haydon

"Battleground State, or In an interview with Dawne Gee, Mayor Greg Fischer says his hands are tied regarding the murder of Breonna Taylor." and "On Finding a Crisp Apple in Louisville's West End" previously published in *TAUNT*.

David Higdon
"Ceramic Jesus" previously published in *Still: The Journal*.

John James
"Kentucky, September" first published in *DIAGRAM*.
"Years I've Slept Right Through" first published in *Harpur Palate*.
"The Milk Hours" first published in *Louisville Review,* reprinted on *Poets.org*.
All three poems appear in *The Milk Hours* (Milkweed Editions, 2019).

Ellen Birkett Morris
"Where There Is Smoke" and "Sport of Kings" previously published in *Abide* (Seven Kitchens Press, 2021).

Nguyễn Vũ Ngọc Uyên
"My South End" previously published in *TAUNT*.

Robert L. Penick
"Midnight at the Quarterpole Bar and Lounge" previously published in *January Review*.

Joy Priest
"Derby" first published by *Drunken Boat* (now *ANMLY*).
"Winning Colors, 1988" first published by *The Rumpus*.
"Abecedarian for Alzheimer's" first published by *PUBLIC POOL*.
"Derby," "Winning Colors, 1988," and "Abecedarian for Alzheimer's" also appear in *Horsepower* (University of Pittsburgh Press, 2020).
"Denial Is a Cliff We Are Driven Over" first published by the Academy of American Poets' Poem-a-Day.

Ryan Ridge
"Drunk and Longing in Louisville" previously published in *New Bad News* (Sarabande Books, 2020).

THANK YOU

Kristen Renee Miller—for your imagination, which encouraged a larger version of my vision for gathering Louisville poets. Thankful to you for conceptualizing this project with me.

Louisville Poets—to you: you who submitted work to this anthology, every poet who is gathered here and every poet who isn't.

Crystal Wilkinson—for your early support of me as a writer, my poetry mama, and our beloved poet laureate. Thank you for talking to me at the beginning of this project and for your insight into the Louisville poetry scene in the '80s and '90s.

Minda Honey—for helping me stay connected to the Louisville writing community, inviting me to teach at Spalding, and lending your time, support, and efforts to this project as an inaugural cohort member of the Curate Purchase Inspire program from Louisville Visual Art.

Fund for the Arts—for offering matching donations to this project through your ArtsMatch for Racial Equity Program and for understanding and believing in the crucial importance of arts as "the soul of our city," which is a huge notion behind this anthology.

National Endowment for the Arts and Inprint Houston—thank you for providing gracious fellowships and institutional support that supported my time and space to put this project together while I was living on a PhD student's salary.

The teachers and communities that instilled a Black community-driven, service ethos in me—my father, Greater Friendship Missionary Baptist Church of Louisville, Kentucky, my coaches at Semple Elementary, Noe

Middle, and Central High, my sensei Nikky Finney, the Affrilachian Poets, and Alpha Kappa Alpha Sorority, Inc.

Nikky Finney—a special thanks to you for enlightening me to the idea that being a poet is a community role, a way to be useful to one's community, and that is has "less to do with inspiration and more to do with wanting to offer something, made with my own two hands, to the people I cherish. . . with wanting poetry to be seen as useful—useful as a roof or coat" (*Scalawag*).

Sarabande Books—for being a phenomenal, warm, and patient team, for your constant enthusiasm around this project every step of the way. Danika Isdahl, Joanna Englert, and Natalie Wollenzien—I loved working with you so much! Thank you for your superior work and gracious spirits. Finally, to Sarabande's founder Sarah Gorham—thank you for your work with literature in our beloved state and city, and for believing in this book.

*Thank you to the individual donors who contributed to the 2021
Fund for the Arts ArtsMatch campaign and thank you to Fund
for the Arts and the LG&E and KU Foundation for providing a
platform for community driven support.*

David Anderson
Margaret Bender-Zanoni
Chad Bennett
Emily Bingham and Stephen Reily
Nora Bonner
Aubrie Cox Warner and Jim Warner
Jamie Cox
Erik Eaker and John Brooks
Nancy Haiman
Daniel Handler and Lisa Brown
Karen Harryman and Kirker Butler
Alice Holbrook
Owen Horton
John James
Nancy Lang
Erin McCoy
Jenny Molberg
Ryan Ridge
Alice Sebold
Eric Shoemaker
Jamey Temple
Ken Walker
Cia White
Doreen Wirsig
Marianne Worthington

Joy Priest is the author of *Horsepower* (Pitt Poetry Series, 2020), selected as the winner of the Donald Hall Prize for Poetry by the nineteenth US Poet Laureate Natasha Trethewey. She is the recipient of a 2021 National Endowment for the Arts fellowship and a 2019–2020 Fine Arts Work Center fellowship, and the winner of the Stanley Kunitz Memorial Prize from the *American Poetry Review*. Her poems have appeared or are forthcoming in numerous publications, including the Academy of American Poets' *Poem-a-Day* series, *The Atlantic*, and *Kenyon Review* among others, as well as in commissions for the Museum of Fine Arts, Houston (MFAH) and the Los Angeles County Museum of Art (LACMA).

Sarabande Books is a nonprofit literary press founded in Louisville, Kentucky. Established in 1994 to champion poetry, fiction, and essay, we are committed to creating lasting editions that honor exceptional writing. With over two hundred titles in print, we have earned a dedicated readership and a national reputation as a publisher of diverse forms and innovative voices.